D1602279

THE HIGH HARD ONE

THE HIGH

WITH MARTIN QUIGLEY

HARD ONE

by Kirby Higbe

New York
THE VIKING PRESS

To THE BROOKLYN FANS AND TO THE GAME OF BASE-
BALL, WHICH HAS DONE SO MUCH FOR SO MANY AND IS A
VITAL PART OF THE HERITAGE OF THIS GREAT COUNTRY OF
OURS.

I WOULD BE REMISS IF I FAILED TO EXPRESS MY APPRE-
CIATION TO THE AMERICAN LEGION FOR GIVING ME AN
OPPORTUNITY TO BE A PART OF THIS GREAT HERITAGE.

K. H.

First published in 1967 by The Viking Press, Inc.
625 Madison Avenue, New York, N.Y. 10022

Published simultaneously in Canada by
The Macmillan Company of Canada Limited

Library of Congress catalog card number: 67–20295
Printed in U.S.A.

Contents

THE HIGH HARD ONE

THE WARM—UP

1

Throwing Rocks

I developed my strong right arm early in life by getting in rock fights and by making bets I could throw rocks farther than anybody thought any boy ever could. I didn't know then that in later life my right arm would be my sole means of support.

I never had much schooling. Things have changed a lot since I was a boy. Back then it seemed like a husky, willing kid could get along all right, the way people always had, without much more than a grade-school education. Now I see, the way the world has changed, that quitting school was the biggest mistake I made, but, tell the truth about it, I didn't have too much choice.

I was born in Columbia, South Carolina, April 8, 1915. The first thing I remember was about two and a half years later: my father taking us to Jacksonville,

Florida, to get away from the flu epidemic. But after a few days he found out it was just as bad there as back home. Before we could get away, the whole family was down with flu, all with high fevers. It was really hell for two weeks. It looked for a while like the whole family would be wiped out. My brother Harold, the youngest at that time, died after about a week. That left my older brother, Lloyd, and me. We came on back to Columbia, all of us still a little sick, and buried my brother. It was a sad time for all of us.

My father in those days was a glass-blower at Lauren's Glass Works, which was having a rough time of it. The company had to pay the employees in stock, or pay them part stock and part cash, every payday. Today it is a big outfit, a large producer of Coca-Cola bottles. A few years ago, after my mother died, we came across some stock notes it had paid my dad in the hard years, but they were no good any more.

After a few more years as a glass-blower, Dad started traveling for the company, selling mostly soft-drink bottles. I was about seven and used to make some trips with him. There was a colored man, Nathan Green, that traveled with Dad to help when we had car trouble, and we did most of the time, and to help in the broken-bottle business. He was a kind of foreman of the other Negroes that worked for my dad.

I never will forget one trip. Dad picked up a hitchhiker—he never passed up a one—who got in the back seat beside old Nathan and started right away asking questions about Dad's business and how much money he carried. He wanted to know whether Nathan was a hitchhiker or a friend of Dad's and kept pressing like that. This fellow rode with us about a hundred miles. When he finally got out, Nathan told my dad his arm was so tired from the tight grip he had on the big monkey wrench beside him that he could hardly raise it. He said if that man had tried to hold us up, he was going to let him have that big old monkey wrench over the head. My dad showed Nathan he had a .38 pistol on the seat beside him. He said he liked to help anybody he could but didn't want anybody hurting him. If that man had tried anything, he wouldn't have hurt anybody else ever again.

Dad used to buy broken glass from bottlers all over the state for shipment back to the glassworks. He kept a crew of ten to twenty men busy cleaning the bottle tops and other trash out of it. While dad was selling new bottles, old Nathan would check the broken glass and load it for shipment. In those days, before everything was automatic, there was always work like that people who didn't know much else could find to do.

I had the sweetest, greatest mother in all the world. She brought all of her children up in Sunday school and church. I don't think there ever was a time that the doors of the good old Tabernacle Baptist Church on Gregg Street were open that she wasn't there with all the kids.

When times were hard, Mama would always encourage us and say God would see us through. He never promised us riches, but He would see us through. She never preached to us but lived the kind of life so that anybody that came in contact with her knew where she stood and was better for knowing her.

I was sickly from the time I got the flu in Jacksonville until I was twelve, and she was always by my side when I needed her. I have certainly missed her. I could always go to her when I had troubles, and she would understand. I gave her my share of her worries, but it is like the old song says, "You always hurt the one you love"—to which I always add a few words of my own: "Because nobody else gives a damn."

Maybe it was from being sickly as a small boy, but I guess you could say that I was my grandmother's (my mother's mother's) favorite grandchild. She was the head of the sewing room in the Columbia Hospital. She used to go to Augusta, Georgia, about three times a year to see her son, and she would take me along every time. I sure did enjoy riding those old steam-engine trains with the cinders flying all over everything. We would have a great time eating lunch on the train. She made ham sandwiches, potato salad, and fried chicken. What a picnic!

Then there was my grandfather (my father's father), who was from up North but he came South and fought for the Confederate Army. It seems that his family had a good deal of money, but he ran away from home when he was fourteen. One of my relatives, an aunt, once went North to Cleveland, Ohio, and talked to some Higbees there that owned the Higbee Department Store and they said they believed he must be their brother that ran away and dropped an *e* off his name.

I used to go to my grandfather's house. He kept his knives as sharp as a razor and could carve anything out of wood. He would make walking canes with figures carved in them, and monkeys out of peach stones, make out of wood fans that would open and shut, most anything. I would ask him what he was doing, and he would say, "Son, I'm just whittling." And he would tell me about the Civil War. He said they would be nearly starving to death and he would volunteer to go across the Northern lines to try and find food for his company.

On one of these expeditions he got shot right above his left knee. They wanted to cut his leg off between the knee and the hip. He begged the doctor not to take it off, but the doctor was going to do it. The general came just at the right time and told the doctor, "If Higbe don't want that leg off, don't do it." The doctor said, "If I don't, he's going to die." My grandfather said, "Leave it, for I would rather be dead than have only one leg." Grandpa always had a limp the rest of his life.

He used to tell me about the time they overran the Northern lines and found some coffee and hardtack. They cooked the coffee and put the hardtack in the coffee to soften it, and worms came to the top.

I said, "Did you drink the coffee?"

He said, "We sure did. Them worms was the only meat we had seen in six months."

He became Chief of Police in Columbia. He never carried a gun. They tell how Grandpa once arrested a big strong drunk who wanted to give him trouble. Grandpa slapped him with a backhand and threw him across his shoulders and started to walk to jail with him. This big fellow grabbed a picket fence and wouldn't let go. Grandpa never stopped walking. He took both the drunk and the fence to jail.

He died when I was still a small boy. I stayed at his house all night the last ten days he lived. He died of cancer of the throat. He suffered quite a bit but he never grumbled. He used to tell me that nobody who had went through the Civil War and survived should ever kick about anything in life, and he never did.

On Hampton Street, not more than five blocks from where I was born and raised, stands the home where President Woodrow Wilson lived as a boy when his father was a minister. Across the street is the Civil War home of Mary Chesnut, who wrote *A Diary from Dixie*, where President Jefferson Davis visited during the War. Hampton Street was named after General Wade Hampton, the great Southern cavalry leader. His family own and operate the largest newspaper in South Carolina, *The State of Columbia*. Gregg Street, one block from Cherokee Street, where I lived, was named after Maxey Gregg, who was killed at the battle of Fredericksburg. So I grew up in poverty but with a wealth of heritage and traditions. I am proud that my grandfather knew the great people that were a part of my neighborhood.

In those early years I had an older brother, L. W. Higbe, Jr., and a younger sister, Cynthia. All my brother was thinking about was going to school and being a doctor, and all I was thinking about was after school and playing baseball. My brother had asthma so bad I could hear him breathing a block from home. He ran into a doctor at the Eagle's Club that had been kicked out of the medical profession. He told my brother that a shot of morphine would ease the hard breathing. So my brother would take a shot of morphine when he had an attack. It eased the pain and made a dope addict out of the patient. He had a rough time of it from the time he started until he died in 1946.

He was in the government hospital in Lexington four times. He sat on my bed many a night and told me the whole time he was in the hospital taking the cure all he thought about was getting out and getting more dope. Twice, before he went in the hospital, he put a dozen pills inside a finger stall, which is a thin rubber thing that fits over the finger, and swallowed them and then got them out of the stool when he was in the hospital. He said when you were going off the stuff cold turkey, it was the worst hell you could ever go through. The reason he went to the hospital was so he could start over again on small doses when he got out and work himself back up to as high as 13 grains a day, enough to kill most people.

He had a fine family and two nice boys, one of them named after me. Later, when I was playing ball, I tried to help Lloyd any way I could, and I would do the same thing over again under the same circumstances. He was smart and a good student and a good-looking boy, and we were real pals.

My sister grew into a real good-looking young lady. She is now Mrs. Earl Buff, the mother of five children, and lives in Columbia.

Later I had another brother, Fraser, who was nine years younger than me. I had already started playing ball before he got started in school good. He was a good student and became the Clerk of Court for Columbia before he was twenty and stayed with it until a few years ago. He said he saw so much trouble he just had to get out of it. He now has a good job with Greyhound Bus Company with headquarters in Atlanta.

I went to the first grade at the old Taylor School, but I had pneumonia for six weeks and failed my first year. I transferred to McMaster School and finished my grammar-school education.

I was a real puny kid, so I started cutting trees and logs all over the countryside, both to build myself up and to make some money. In those days all the people in the country needed wood both for their cookstoves and to heat with. I would walk out in the country, sometimes a good many miles, and cut wood all day for 25 cents and a good country meal. They really put out some good country food. Cutting wood with a 12-pound ax gives you a good appetite.

The first ball I played was in the street. You could buy a ball for a dime, which was the most we ever had, but you hit it good once or twice and you would have to go look for friction tape. We would wrap the balls so much you could hardly pick them up, let alone hit them. We finally got smart and would go to the store and slip a dollar ball in the dime box of balls and hand it to the girl with a dime. A dollar ball would last us three or four days. Then we would go back and switch balls again.

Before I played American Legion ball, we would pick up a team and go to the South Carolina Penitentiary, which was not far from our neighborhood, and play the Caged Tigers at high noon every Saturday. Then we would go down and play a mill team at 3 P.M. I would pitch both games. If we could have found a third team to play that day, I would have been glad to pitch that game too.

I have walked five or six miles many a time to play a ball game. We had to walk where we went.

From my house, which was in a middle-class neighborhood where a lot of railroad men lived, to get to school we either had to go four or five blocks out of our way around the Bottoms, or right through it. The Bottoms was a colored neighborhood. If you are in Columbia and staying at the Town House, which they say is one of the most beautiful motels in the country and is built where General Sheridan made his headquarters during the Federal occupation of Columbia, you walk around to the back and you will be standing on top of the steep red clay bank that leads down to the Bottoms. It's still there like it was in those days.

We knew if we went across the Bottoms we would have to fight our way through with rocks. The colored kids were waiting for us with rocks. It was their Bottoms. So we would always fill our pockets with rocks when we left home because there wasn't time to look for rocks when we got there. When we hit the Bottoms, the rocking started. We would have to throw rocks from the time we entered until the time we got to the top of that steep clay bank. When it was raining, that bank was so slick you would go up two steps and fall back three with the rocks sailing over your head like bullets.

I was on radio one time with Bill Stern in New York, and he asked me how I ever got such a strong arm. I told him throwing rocks at Negroes, and he cut me off the mike right away. I don't think he understood.

We were Southern boys, brought up to believe in the separation of the races, but we didn't hate Negroes. The rock fights were more of a game on both sides. It was a challenge on both sides. They threw as many rocks as we did, sometimes more, being on their home field, so to speak, and not having to scramble up that clay bank. In those days different kinds of kids had fights like that all over the country. Up North it might be the Irish against the Germans, or the Poles against the Swedes, but with us it was against the colored kids. In the big cities up North, like in Brooklyn, where I played ball so long, the kid gangs got really vicious and used more weapons than rocks on each other.

When they were building the nurses' home at Columbia Hospital nearby, one night after school we got in a rock fight where the construction was taking place. There were lots of rocks and places to take cover. The fight lasted until daylight.

I believe that throwing rocks as a boy was the reason I did have such a strong arm and could pitch every day.

When the depression hit, we had a rough time of it, but we were a family that was real close, and there wasn't anything we wouldn't do for each other. My mother went to work in a sewing room at about $12 a week. There was plenty of times we ate potato sandwiches, and I mean that is all. When we had a little fatback for supper, that was a feast. Many times we had to use kerosene to see by because we couldn't pay the light bill.

After grammar school I went one year to Wardlaw Junior High School, where I got more practice for my baseball career. There was a pretty good-sized field behind the school, about 300 feet from home plate to the center-field fence. Money was so scarce the only way I could eat was bet 10 or 15 cents I could throw the ball over the center-field fence from home plate. That is the way I ate lunch the whole year at Wardlaw.

My father was sick and what my mother was making in the sewing room wasn't enough, and I was strong then and wasn't interested in school. I guess it was the biggest mistake of my life, but I quit school after the seventh grade, when I was fourteen, and went to work at the Southern Railroad as a messenger boy at $50 a month.

There was an old hotel about a hundred yards from the station. I used to bet the railroad men ten cents that I could throw a rock over the hotel from the station. I never lost a bet, and after about thirty days the word got around to the railroad men that came in there, and none of them would give me a bet. For the rest of the time I worked at the railroad, I used to throw rocks over that hotel for thirty minutes a day. I never had a sore arm in my life.

2

Throwing the Ball

In 1931, after I left the railroad, I went to work for Claussen's Bakery to cut rolls by hand and to pitch on the baseball team. The first Saturday, in what was my first real baseball game, I pitched a one-hitter against a pretty good semi-pro team, and we won, 11–0. After working another week cutting rolls by hand, I came up with blisters on both hands. I don't think I got anybody out after that.

Columbia Post 6 of the American Legion had started a baseball team the year before, and some of the men behind it heard that I could throw hard and asked me to try out for it. I did and was picked as one of the pitchers.

Most of the boys were from the same neighborhood and had been playing pick-up ball together for four or five years, which had a good deal to do with our success. Getting ready for the American Legion junior baseball tournament, one loss and out, we played the semi-pro teams around Columbia made up of older fellows, and we held our own against them.

Our first baseman was a pal from the rock-fight days, K. K. Ouzts, who later played pro ball. I've lost track of Aaron Koleske, who was at second base. Harry Laval at short was the son of the head football coach at the University of Southern California. Runt Elliott was at third. Jim Good, our left fielder, became an FBI agent. Bee Harper, in center, is now in the real-estate business in Columbia. Our right fielder, Horace Womack, has a son, Dooley, who is now a relief pitcher for the Yankees. The other two pitchers were J. J. "Country" Kneece and Dick McCreary, now an insurance executive in Columbia. Kneece later signed with the Boston Red Sox and pitched three straight shut-outs in the old Piedmont League. Then he quit playing ball and went back to school. Today he is a buyer for a big mill in Spartanburg, South Carolina. Our catchers were J. W. "Hook" Williamson and Bunny Graham. Our two utility players were Roy Faust, now a captain on the police force in Anderson, South Carolina, and Richard Taliaferro, one of the leading surgeons in Greensboro, North Carolina.

We drove to Sumter for our first tournament game in three cars. One was driven by our coach, Paul Autry, one by our athletic officer, Laurens Hamilton, and the third by Dr. Hayden, a dentist in Columbia who, with his wife, Ada, was like father and mother to the whole club.

We beat hell out of Sumter and traveled all over the

state, including Union, Elloree, Spartanburg, Green-
ville, St. Matthews, Winnsboro, Clinton, and Whitmore,
and went through them all like a dose of salts. Then we
played Charleston for the state championship. Country
Kneece went all the way, eleven innings, and we won
2–1. Little Bee Harper (who is now coach of the Columbia Legion team) stole six bases, scored both runs, and
covered center field like the dew covers Dixie.

We had a week to practice for the regionals, but we
didn't do anything special to get ready. We did what
we did anyway—played baseball all day long.

The tournament was in Gastonia, North Carolina, and
this time we went in a bus, like professional ballplayers.
We were cocky and didn't think anybody in the world
could beat us.

In our first game, against Gastonia, which had six
left-handed hitters in the line-up, our coach started our
first baseman, K. K. Ouzts, a left-hander who could
throw bullets. But those left-hand hitters must not of
known the percentage was against them because they
scored five runs and had two men on base, and there
was still nobody out in the first inning.

So Coach Autry called on me. "Hig," he said, "you
better get in there and stop 'em and give our hitters
a chance to catch up." They didn't score any more,
but they had us 5–3 going into the ninth. We had men
on first and second with two outs, and I thought we
were gone for sure, because Jim Good, our left fielder,
was up and he hadn't hit much all year. But he hit a
triple that tied the game, and then damn if he didn't
steal home, and we beat them 6–5.

Next day, against Roanoke Rapids, we had to play
catch-up ball again when they got four runs off Country

Kneece in the first inning. But he held them from there, and we went into the ninth down 4–2. We got the bases loaded with two out, and who the hell you think was the hitter but Jim Good. And damn if he don't hit another triple and win for us 5–4.

We went on to win them all and the regional championship, and a week later we were on our way to Manchester, New Hampshire, for the sectionals. Gastonia was the farthest any of us ever had been away from home, and we had gone there on a bus. We left Columbia at noon on a Sunday in a Pullman car, big-league.

Eating in the diner, I said to myself, "Boy, this is really living," and I made up my mind right then and there that I was going to be a big-league ballplayer. I knew that nothing could stop me; I was headed for the big leagues.

We had about six hours' layover in New York, and they took us sightseeing. New York looked like the whole world rolled into one city. They took us to Central Park, Chinatown, and to the top of the Empire State Building. Damn if I could hardly see the ground. The cars looked like flies crawling on a watermelon rind.

On the train to Manchester we went through mountains, and they impressed me, a sight to behold, almost as much as New York.

The first game we beat Jackson, Mississippi, with Country pitching, in an easy game, 5–1. I pitched the next day against Bridgeport, Connecticut, the favorites to win. They were the biggest team we had seen. Most of them shaved and had names I couldn't pronounce, let alone spell. We were down 1–0 in the fourth, and I came to bat with two on and one out and hit the ball over the center fielder's head. Both runners scored easily, but my jockey strap broke between first and second and I had to run sideways into third for a hard triple on what should have been an easy home run. We won it 5–3, with most of the big crowd pulling for us because we were the underdogs.

Country set down Manchester in the finals, 9–2, and we were the happiest bunch of kids you ever saw as we headed all the way to Houston, Texas, five days on the train, for the Little World Series. We stopped off to play a practice game at Indianapolis, where the American Legion had its headquarters. They beat us, and I didn't like it. I don't care what contest you are in, the hell with losing.

They gave all us boys a dollar a day spending money while we were traveling. It was the most money any of us had ever had to spend. In Houston they put us up at the Rice Hotel, which was a grander place than we knew there was.

We were playing South Chicago, Illinois, for the world's junior championship, two out of three. When they came on the field, I thought it was the Houston club from the Texas League, they looked that big. The first game was a night game. We had never even seen a night game. Some of the folks that came from Columbia asked our coach to pitch me that night game because I was faster than Kneece, but Coach Autry said, "I have taken them this far, and I'll run the ball club like I see fit." And Country pitched.

They beat hell out of us, 13–4, but we still thought we could take them.

It was 102 degrees in the shade next day, but we weren't playing in the shade. There were fifteen thousand people in the stands, the most people I had ever seen in one place, and it seemed like they was all pulling for us because we had got beat so bad the night before.

I was nervous when I warmed up. I don't believe I ever started a ball game in all my years that I wasn't nervous. But after the first pitch to the first batter, everything was okay. This was it. We had been playing three and a half months, and I thought: Let's don't come all this way to lose it now.

I never saw a game with so many goose eggs on the scoreboard.

In the sixth, we got men on first and third with one out. Our squeeze play got messed up, and the runner from third was tagged out at home. The next batter hit a fly ball to center, but instead of bringing a run home, it was just another third out.

In the eighth, our lead-off man hit a double, and the next man sacrificed him to third, but he died there.

I weighed 140 pounds when I took the field, and I didn't have too much to spare, but I kept bearing down and the sweat kept running off me.

In the top of the fourteenth they scored a run on an error, and we couldn't match it, and the season was over.

Through all my baseball career, big leagues and all, it was the toughest game I ever lost. I had given it everything I had for three and a half hours and was down to 126 pounds. I cried like a baby after the game.

The winning team got a free trip to the World Series, and all I could think of was that I had lost the game.

It took us three nights and two days to get back to Columbia. There were five thousand people waiting for us at the depot.

THE GAME

1

Starting Out

Losing that ball game was the end of my boyhood. In the morning and from then on I began thinking about baseball as the main business of my life. You can't see ahead. You go a pitch at a time, an inning at a time, one game at a time.

After the American Legion season in 1931, I was contacted by four or five big-league scouts, but I had always thought of the Pittsburgh Pirates as my team because they had a farm team in Columbia in the old Sally League. So when they offered a $500 bonus and $300 a month to play ball, I thought I was already a millionaire. Some of the boys I knew were playing in the Cardinal farm system, which was then known as the Cardinal Chain Gang, for $50 to $75 a month. So I signed with the Pirates for the 1932 season and was sent to Tulsa in the old Texas League.

I took the bus to Bartlesville, Oklahoma, where they had spring training, and I passed my seventeenth birthday there. It was the first time I had been away from home on my own.

The manager was Art Griggs, a rough-and-tumble fellow but a real good man. He and his wife watched out for me as best they could and treated me like a son. I thought a lot of Don Stewart, the secretary, too. The other players were older than me. Most of them didn't have much more education than me but were poor rough boys who didn't have, or want, any other way of making a living in those Depression years than playing ball. Their parents didn't have any way of sending them on to school, and there wasn't a college man among us nor too many that had finished up their high school. They played hard ball and to win, and they lived hard too.

I was in good shape and worked real hard. I could really throw hard and had a good curve but didn't know a damn about pitching, though I thought I did, and I was wild. I could always get them out when I got the ball over the plate, but even my own ballplayers was scared to hit against me in batting practice. We had a big outfielder named Stan Schino who could hit the ball a country mile, but I put him out of commission for two weeks with a fast ball that broke his ribs. So old Art said, "Hig, you'll just have to throw on the sidelines until your control improves."

About a week later Art let me start in an exhibition game against Omaha, and I was tickled for the chance. I struck the first man out, and I said, "Hig, you are ready for the big leagues already." But I hit the next batter in the back, and Pug Griffin, the Omaha manager, was the third batter. He got his name because he looked just like one of those old English bulldogs and was mean as hell. Damn if I didn't hit him in the ribs and break a few. I walked the next guy and hit the fifth batter. Pug marched up to old Art and told him, "You get that boy out of there, or I'll call the game. Sending hitters up against a wild man like that is worse than sending the whole club off to war." So old Art took me out, and that was the only game I ever appeared in for the Tulsa ball club.

I stayed on through spring training and went to Tulsa with them. About then I started having fun dating girls and taking a few drinks along with the others. In Tulsa I started going out with a cute little Indian girl. One morning, about 3 A.M., when I was supposed to be long in bed, I went in the basement entrance and rang for the elevator there so I would not have to go through the lobby, but the elevator stopped at the first floor and who the hell had buzzed the buzzer but old Art. He said, "Son, you are up early this morning, and when did they move your room down to the basement? I ought to fine you one hundred dollars but this time I'm going to let you off with a warning and twenty extra laps around the field today." After that I took old Art's advice and curtailed my love life quite a bit and started hanging around the lobby nights. There was a quarter slot machine there. What little money I had I put in the damn thing the first night. So I watched others play and learned that about half the quarters in the jackpot would hang up in the mint rack. The elevator boy was on to it too. So we would stand and wait and hope somebody would hit the jackpot who didn't know you had to turn the handle on the mint rack to get all the quarters. Damn if a fellow didn't hit it. He walked away whistling, and me and the elevator boy took off for the one-armed bandit. While we were rassling to get to the mint handle, one of the bellboys scooted in, turned the knob, and walked away with $15 worth of our quarters.

Being the youngest on the club, they played all kinds of tricks on me. I had the luck to overhear them planning one. They were telling Clay Mahaffey, another South Carolina boy who was a pretty good pitcher and who was my roomie, to make out like he was walking in his sleep and to start choking me. So I made out like I was asleep until about midnight, when Clay got out of bed and started toward my bed. I picked up a chair and started to whack him over the head. He began to holler, "I'm awake, roomie. I'm awake. Put that damn chair down!"

When the club went on the road, old Art left me and a veteran catcher, Dallas Warren, behind so I could work on my control. Dallas didn't live in the hotel, and I began getting homesick, and let me tell you that is the worst sickness there is. After three or four days I couldn't sleep nor eat, and a few days later I called my mother. She sent my brother Lloyd on the bus out to get me. I didn't tell anyone I was leaving the ball club. I just packed my clothes. We hitchhiked back to Columbia in eight days, stopping off to see the 500 in Indianapolis on the way. I was never happier to see old Columbia.

I went down to Barnwell and played semi-pro ball for a few dollars a game in a pretty good league. Graniteville, in the Horse Creek Valley of South Carolina, was a rough town with real baseball fans. I was going to pitch one Saturday afternoon there before a big wild crowd. One guy come up to me before the game and said he was going to kill me if I won that game. It wasn't ten minutes later another fellow said he was going to kill me if I didn't win it. I couldn't figure out how the hell I could get a tie so I said to myself, "Hig, if you're going to die either way, go down winning." I pitched a two-hitter, and we won, 2–0. As soon as I got the last man out, I jumped the hell away from that place.

We had lots of fun in Barnwell. We used to go out and steal us twenty to thirty fine big watermelons and take them down to a swimming hole and plug them and pour corn liquor in them, and go get them after the game.

One night four of us ballplayers went out in the country to a place where we had heard you could get a half-gallon of corn for $2, which was all we had. The place was dark, and the man gave us the jar and took our money. When we got to where there was some light, we saw this big green fly on top of the liquor. We all said we wouldn't drink any of that stuff, but before we got through we were arguing about who was going to squeeze-dry the fly and drink that.

One way we used to keep a player in shape was to ask him if he wanted to go see Maude, a good-looker and really put together. We would have four or five of us with a shotgun in an old empty house out in the country. One of us would drive the player that could use some extra running out there and tell him to go up on the porch and knock and tell whoever answered he had come to see Maude. So he would. Then the man inside with the gun would shoot it off and holler, "So you're the guy that's been fooling around with my wife. I'm gonna get you this time." The guy with the car would act scared and drive off, and the victim would take off across country, twelve miles to town.

Later in the summer my good friend K. K. Ouzts, who had played American Legion ball with me, asked me to go to Anderson, South Carolina, to play ball in a mill league. I was making so little in Barnwell that I didn't even ask what the pay was in Anderson, but I found out right quick. I worked 55 hours a week in the mill at 10 cents an hour for $5.50 a week and pitched for nothing Saturdays and Sundays. My room and board was $2.50 a week, so I had $3 clear to blow as I saw fit.

We could get Wing or Twenty Grand cigarettes for 10 cents a package and couldn't afford them. We would get Hoover dust, which is what we called Golden Grain or Bull Durham, and roll 50 cigarettes for 5 cents.

We had some real good ball games and drew some good crowds at 25 cents a head. We won the pennant and the playoff with a ball club I would say was as good as or better than any club in AA baseball today.

When I got back to Columbia, there was a letter from Tulsa saying they were expecting me to join the club for spring training in 1933. That winter I helped my brother with the bread and paper route he carried every night. We would leave at 12:30 A.M. and make a circle through Sumter, Florence, Parkers Cross Roads, and St. Matthews, 270 miles every night, and be back in Columbia around 7 A.M. But when I drove it by myself I wouldn't get back until 11 A.M. because I would stop off to hunt with a good friend who had a fine bird dog. Trouble was, this dog would fool around for about thirty minutes, and my friend would say, "Hig, it's about time that damn dog started hunting." So he would let the dog get about fifty yards in front of him and let him have it with a blast of bird shot. He would sting hell out of that dog, and then he would start hunting. I guess we went hunting about forty-five times that winter. I used to get lots of complaints from our subscribers because the paper was late, but the hunting with old Ross was worth it.

I went back to spring training with Tulsa. I could throw as hard as anybody that ever lived, but that home plate didn't look any bigger than a postage stamp. After about three weeks, old Art called me in and said, "Hig, it is a damn shame. You can throw harder than anybody I ever seen, but you couldn't hit a barn if you were standing right up against it. I'm going to send you down to Muskegee. Maybe old Rube can do something with you." Old Rube was Rube Marquard, the former pitching great with the Giants.

Rube did all he could, but I was just wild. I would start a game and get them out for two or three innings, and then I would start walking hitters or hitting them and they would say, "Get that wild man out of here or we'll take our ball club off the field." Rube told old Art I had the greatest arm and the worst control he had ever seen. He said, "It's dangerous to be on the same field Hig is pitching on."

When I got back to Tulsa, old Art said, "Hig, you are as free as the birds that fly." One of the players said, "Hig, you ain't a ballplayer until you've been released three or four times." So I went back home and played with another mill team in Laurens, in both the 1933 and 1934 seasons.

Back in those days everybody had the desire. We really wanted to play ball. We went out to win. When you see a team that goes all out to win, you will see a winner most of the time. The same thing goes for a ballplayer with lots of desire. If he has some ability to go with the desire, he will be a real ballplayer. It was just semi-pro ball, but it was good baseball because it was played with the desire.

To play ball in that league, you had to work in the mill all day. I pitched the opening game in Laurens and won it 2–0 and told them it was too rough working in the mill and pitching, so I was quitting. The boss came and put me working outside on the construction gang, which was better. These young ballplayers today, I wonder would they have enough desire to work hard fifty-five hours a week for the chance to play ball.

We had lots of fun, too, going to square dances every Saturday night. After a few drinks of corn, which we would buy for 50 cents a pint, you could really swing.

Most of the players stayed at the same boarding house, and we used to have some real poker games there. One night the police came by and caught us. The old judge was a good baseball man. He fined all seven of us $10 and told us we could pay it by playing good baseball, so much for a home run, so much for a hit with men on, etc. He told me $5 would come off every time I won a game.

"Judge," I said, "I pitch two games every week, so it looks like I will be able to play poker again by Saturday night."

He said, "Well, Higbe, we will just take a dollar off for every game you win. You should win just about ten more this year."

I should have kept my mouth shut while I was ahead.

Old Hig didn't lose many in those days; I used to tell them I was like boiled ham, always ready. My only regret in baseball was that I was not an infielder or an outfielder so I could play every day. I dearly loved baseball.

We won the pennant and the playoff both years I was with Laurens. My control was getting better. At the end of the 1934 season Chick Galloway, a major-league scout, said he wanted to take me down to Atlanta, where they had a month left of the season, for a tryout with the Crackers. I worked out with the club for three days and then they took me down to a little town in Georgia where I pitched for the Bona Allen team, a shoe manufacturer, against Douglas and beat them 3–0, and signed with Atlanta the next day for $500, the most money I'd ever seen.

Up the Baseball Ladder

On the field Spencer Abbott, manager of the Crackers, was a rough and tough wild man, giving every game everything he and his players had, but off the field the nicest fellow you ever saw.

The day after I signed, I went with the club to New Orleans. On the train Joe Palmisano, a catcher, was telling me about the night life there, and when we got there he showed me around. I had never seen champagne before, but I drank more that night than most people ever will see in their whole lives. The strip-tease shows, where they went at it all night, kept my eyes wide open, and the master of ceremonies would come around and remind us we could get a ringside seat after the show for five bucks.

We got back to the hotel about 5 A.M., and Joe said, "Hig, let's get up at seven and let old Spencer see us, and then we'll go back to bed and catch up." The skipper saw us and came to me and said, "Higbe, you are pitching the first game today."

It was a hot day, even for New Orleans. I walked everybody in the ball park and lasted four innings. Back in the clubhouse, the more water I drank, the drunker I got. After the first game, Spencer came to me and said, "Higbe, you are going to start the second game."

I must have walked eighteen men in seven innings, but when I got the ball over, I got them out; but I lost both games. Spencer came to me and said, "You cost me too much money to let you go, but you are too wild to pitch, so I am going to try to make an outfielder out of you."

I didn't play with Atlanta but a month, but I sure learned a lot about baseball and the ways of baseball players.

One of our pitchers was Harry Kelly, who had played in the Southern League ten years and had won twenty games or more for about seven of those years. But Spence was always telling him how to pitch. One day, before a game with Chattanooga, Harry spoke up and said, "Skip, I think I know these hitters better'n you do." Spence said, "All right, Kelly, you pitch them your way and we'll see what happens."

Harry pitched shut-out ball until he gave up a run in the bottom of the eighth, and they were leading 1–0. When he came in for the top of the ninth, Harry sat down and a 16-pound shot-put came crashing beside him in the dugout, just missing his head. After heaving it, Spence hollered, "From now on, Kelly, you pitch the way I tell you."

We lost the first game of a doubleheader to Little Rock 3–2 in eleven innings. The second game went into the eleventh tied 2–2. They had a man on second with two outs, and the next hitter drove him in with the winning run, and we all went to the shower. But Spencer wasn't there. When that ball was hit, Spencer jumped up so mad he hit his head on the top of the dugout and knocked himself out. He finally showed up with a big bump on his head.

There was a big outfielder we called the Prince on the club, who seemed to have ten or twelve girls in every town. Spence would have him tailed and would catch him and fine him $100 three or four times a month. Then he would lend him the money to pay the fines and end up the only loser.

One night in Memphis, the Prince came into the lobby with *three* girls. Spence suspended him for the rest of the season on the spot. The next day at the ball park Spence asked where the Prince was, and we reminded him he was through for the season. "The Prince knows I was only kidding," Spence said. "Send to the hotel and get him."

The Prince was a great ballplayer. He would hit a ball 400 feet and say, "I didn't get good wood on it." He drove in a hundred runs every year and had a great arm. He played hard all the time, on the field and off. No wonder Spence was so crazy about him.

The ball park in Nashville, Sulphur Dell, was built on an old dump. Every time we went there, all the pitchers got sick, either from the short right-field fence, the line-up of good left-handed hitters, or the smell. Under Charlie Dressen, Nashville won the pennant easy that year, and Atlanta finished fourth.

I went to spring training in Daytona Beach, thinking I had the club made, at last I was on my way to the big leagues, but about a week before we broke camp Spence came to me and said, "Hig, I am sending you to Portsmouth." That was in the old Piedmont League, and the manager there was Pip Koehler, who I had met on the Atlanta club the year before. He was a real good fellow and the best hit-and-run man I had ever seen. He put me back to pitching. He said, "Hig, you are going to pitch for me if you walk everybody in the state of Virginia."

Our last exhibition game that spring was with the Kansas City Blues, in the AAA American Association. They had a lot of players that in a few years were to be busting fences for the Yankees. We gave them a pretty good game for four or five innings, and then they began hitting me pretty good. I remembered we had some baseballs we had kept in the icebox all winter to keep them fresh for the new season. I told Pip that we might could get them out if he would ring in some of those snowballs. So he gave some to the umpire. You should have seen those power hitters swinging from the heels and hitting the ball on the nose for a soft fly in the infield. If I could have pitched those icebox balls all the time, I wouldn't have needed anything else.

At Portsmouth there was a cute-looking girl that came to our games all the time. I had my eye on her and she on me, and finally the night came. We took off after the game to Norfolk across the bay, where we had a doubleheader the next day. I told the bellboy to be sure and call me at nine, because I had to get back to Portsmouth, get in uniform, and be back in Norfolk by noon. The boy forgot, and I didn't wake up until twelve-thirty. I rushed to Portsmouth, got my uniform on, and got back to Norfolk just in time for the second inning of the second game. Pip was playing the outfield, so I took his place coaching third like nothing had happened. It was lucky for me we had won the first game. I figured that if we could win the second game, old Pip wouldn't be too hard on me, so I gave it all I had coaching on third. We won them both and he said, "Hig, maybe you better try being late more often." Then he said, "You are pitching tomorrow and if you don't pitch nine innings and win, it will cost you one hundred dollars."

I could really hum that pea about then, and I won the next day 1–0 in ten innings. After the game I told Pip I thought I had another night out coming.

Pip used to tell me I was winning ball games but giving him ulcers. I would walk three and then strike out three. The opposing teams would leave at least fifteen men on base every game, and I would be the winner. I would usually walk twelve to fourteen men and strike out fourteen to sixteen.

In Portsmouth we stayed at the YMCA, where there was just one bathroom on each floor. One outfielder who roomed next to me had weak kidneys and used to have to go every night. He kept asking the room clerk to move him closer to the toilet, but the clerk had his own ideas. This fellow couldn't make it to the toilet so he would go right out the window. When the clerk got caught in a one-stream rain one night, he moved him next to the toilet.

We used to hang around the drugstore and lots of good-looking girls would come there and flirt around and talk, and we had a lot of fun. We played rough, and many funny things that happened were funny only afterward when it turned out nobody got killed.

The bus rides were the worst thing about the minor leagues. When we went on a road trip we would leave right after a ball game, ride all night, and get to the next town in time to put on our uniforms and start playing ball. The rough trip was the one from Portsmouth to Asheville, North Carolina. The next day's pitcher would get to stretch out in the overhead luggage rack, which we called the upper berth. You would be just about asleep, going around those mountain curves, when a sharp turn would throw you out of the rack and down to the aisle. I must have taken that fall a dozen times that year. Instead of warming up after one of those rides, I would try to get one of the players to give me a rubdown. We didn't have a trainer.

About the middle of the season I began to lose what little control I had, and Pip said, "Hig, I'm going to send you down to a semi-pro club at Newbern, North Carolina, for a couple of weeks to help you get your control back."

I pitched a shut-out for them my first game, and then Richmond in the Piedmont League came down to play us, and I shut them out on two hits.

Eddie Rommel, the old Athletics pitcher, was managing the Richmond Club, and he wanted to know what I was doing down there. When I told him he said, "They can't farm you out to a semi-pro team. That's the same as giving you your release. I will give you one thousand dollars to sign with our club."

About three days later Pip brought the Portsmouth team down, and damn if I didn't shut them out on two hits and win 1–0.

Pip said, "Pack your clothes, Hig, you're going back to Portsmouth with us."

"I'm going to sign with Richmond for a thousand dollars," I told him.

He called the owner and came back and said, "Hig, I'll give you a hundred dollars to come back and a hundred dollars a month raise."

All I wanted to do was get in the big leagues, and I figured Portsmouth gave me the best shot at it, so back I went to the all-night bus rides. We finished fourth, and I won ten and lost thirteen. My control had got better—on the field, that is.

During the winter I had quite a few colds and couldn't get my weight up past 140 pounds. The doctor said my tonsils were bad and had to come out. I was in the hospital for ten days and was slow coming around. So when the season started, Portsmouth lent me to Columbia in the Sally League so I could work out with them. I pitched a few games for them and began to pick up, and then Portsmouth recalled me. Playing ball that summer, I gained 40 pounds and got up close to my best weight of 190.

What I remember best about playing with Columbia was hitting the longest ball that ever has been hit, up to today, out of that park. It went clear over the center-field flagpole.

The Chicago Cubs had a working agreement with Portsmouth under which they sent players there and in return had the right to buy any two players from them. At the end of the 1936 season with Portsmouth, the Cubs took me, and I thought, Hig, you're in the big leagues at last.

I went out West to spring training with the Cubs in

1937 and stayed right through until we got back to Chicago for the final spring series against the White Sox. In all the years I had been playing ball, I had never seen a game in a major-league park until we went to Comiskey Park for that series. The first one I saw, I played in.

There was a crowd of about 40,000 there. I went in to pitch the last four innings with the score tied 1–1.

I thought I was dreaming, pitching in a major-league park, finishing a game for one of the greatest pitchers of all time. I guess that's why I pitched so good that day. They only got one hit off me, and we beat them 3–1. It was a real good day for Monty too. He got quite a haul.

I thought I had it made in the big leagues after that game, but two days later, Charlie Grimm called me in and said, "Hig, you've got major-league stuff, but you need more seasoning." And he said he was sending me down to Moline in the Three-I league. He said, "Have a good year, and we will bring you up at the end of the season."

That really hurt, because I thought I was ready. I'd been playing ball a long time, all my life, it seemed, getting ready.

I remembered Jim Lindsey, a fine left-handed pitcher I was with in Atlanta. Jim said that he once had a talk with Branch Rickey, when Mr. Rickey was head of the Cardinal Chain Gang. Mr. Rickey told him, "Jim, you've got a world of stuff, but you don't have the experience to be a major-league pitcher, so I'm going to leave you in the minor leagues to season." He left him there about seven years and called him up and told him, "Jim, you're one of the most seasoned and experienced pitchers we've got, but you just don't have major-league stuff." Jim went on, though, to show him he was a major-league pitcher for a good many years.

In baseball that's the way it is. A player goes where he is sent. I went to Moline.

Mike Gazella was the manager at Moline. He had played with Babe Ruth and the Yankees. He used to tell stories about the Babe, like the time he nailed a player's shoes to the clubhouse floor, and you could hear Babe laughing about it all over town. But when this guy cut the top off Babe's straw hat, the Babe was so mad he wanted to fight everybody on the ball club.

The night before the opening game, which I was supposed to pitch, I went out on the town with another pitcher. He was drinking sloe gin, which I had never seen before. I just had a few nips of wine, about a gallon. When we got home, about 4 A.M., he got sick, and I thought he was bleeding to death. I started to carry him to a doctor. He said, "Roomie, leave me alone. That's just the color of sloe gin." When we got up, I took a big drink of water and was just about as drunk as I was the night before. I was a sick boy, but I pitched the game, and we won it.

One Saturday night in Peoria I went to a late show with about five other fellows. When we left about 1:30 A.M., Mike was right behind us. He said, "Hig, you are going to pitch the whole game tomorrow if you get beat one hundred to nothing." The next day it was about 109 degrees, and I got by the first inning, and then they started hitting the ball hard. About the fourth inning I was through. Old Mike came out and said, "Hig, it is all yours. You are going to pitch the whole game." The game lasted four hours, and we finally beat them 14–12.

Old Mike said, "Nice going, Hig, you really held them close."

One day old Mike asked me to see if I could help get Hal Anderson, a left-hander, to learn to throw harder. He was warming up for a game in front of the grandstand, and I went to him and said, "Hal, just rear back and follow through and throw as hard as you can." Damn if the first one he tried under my coaching didn't shoot up in the box seats and hit the wife of a club official right on the head. I thought he had killed her. Old Mike said, "Hig, just forget it. Every time you start thinking, something bad happens. From now on, don't think. Just throw that ball."

I was throwing against Clinton, Iowa, one night, and throwing hard. I had struck out thirteen in five innings. Clyde Sukeforth, their manager, was telling his hitters to go up there and hit. He said, "I can hit Higbe with one eye closed." In the sixth inning his catcher got in an argument with the plate umpire, and before Clyde could get between them, the catcher was thrown out of the game. So old Clyde, a fine catcher, had to come in to catch. His players said, "Here's your chance, Skip. Close one eye and let's see you hit him." Clyde came up in the seventh with a man on second and two out. I got two quick strikes on him. His boys kept hollering, "Skip, close one eye!" I threw him a high hard one. As he ducked out of the way, the ball hit his bat and went over the third baseman for a base hit.

Clyde said, "Boys, I told you I could hit him with one eye closed."

One of them said, "You done better than that, Clyde, you hit him with both eyes closed."

I had a really fine year, winning 21 and losing 5,

the best record in the league. I walked 141 and struck out 257.

Maybe it was home cooking and getting married that did it for me. Back home during the off-season in Columbia, I had met Anne Ellerbe at a softball game, which I used to play a good deal between baseball seasons, and started dating her. When I left for spring training, I told her I would send for her as soon as I got settled. I called her from Moline and told her to come on. I didn't have much money. In fact, I had to borrow $10 from Frank Hearn, the business manager, to pay the preacher. Frank and his wife stood up for us. I was twenty-one years old.

I had signed a contract with the Cubs for $300 a month. The salary limit in the Three-I League was $150 a month, but if the Cubs recalled me they would have to pay the difference, which would amount to about $800, a hell of a lot of money to us in those days.

Anne knew I had to eat pretty good to stay strong. Damn if she didn't buy pork chops and then cut meat off them for me, and she would gnaw on the bones. She would have rice and stewed tomatoes and other vegetables and was a pretty damn good cook.

On the road our meal allowance was $2 a day, and Mike would give it to us day by day so we wouldn't lose it playing poker. To get your money, you had to either get up by 7 A.M., when old Mike left for his daily round of golf, or leave your door open so he could put it on your bed. Next to baseball itself, old Mike was a golf man. On the road we would eat mostly in cafeterias, and you could eat all you wanted and then some on $2 in those days. There was this one fellow so close with his money he would go through the line and get a glass of iced tea and follow me to my table. He would eat what I would leave. He saved $150 on meal money and weighed just as much as I did at the end of the season.

Chicago called me back up at the end of the season. I joined the Cubs in St. Louis. I pitched my first major-league game in Chicago that year, against the Cardinals at Wrigley Field.

Gabby Hartnett, one of the wisest and best catchers who ever played, was catching for the Cubs. We had them beat 5–0 in the sixth inning, and I was pitching good ball, quite pleased with myself.

Johnny Mize came to bat with one on and one out. Gabby called for the curve three times, and I shook him off three times. Gabby called time and came out to the mound. "Okay, busher," he said, "I am going to let you throw the fast ball, but when you do the score will be five to two."

Big Jawn sure did hit my Sunday fast ball. The last I saw, it was headed over some apartment buildings, and it may be still going. After the game, which I won, Gabby called me over to his locker and said, "Hig, with that good arm of yours, you can be a major-league pitcher, but let me think for you for a while."

The Cubs sent me my contract in February, for $2500 for the year, and I signed it and got ready to go to spring training. I was anxious to get started, but then something happened I never have been able to explain except to say I got homesick. The first start I made I got as far as Knoxville. I got off the train there and went back home. The Cubs called every day and wanted to know when I was coming. The fourth day I was ready to make another start and got as far as Cincinnati before I got off the train and went back home. About four days later, my wife, mother, and brother drove me to Spartanburg to catch the train. I said good-by and got on the train—and got right out on the other side. I caught a bus home and got there just after they got home from seeing me off.

I called the Cubs and asked them to send me to Birmingham, where I would get ready and come to them when they wanted me.

If you have never been homesick, you don't know how it is. It's just like war, you have to be in one to know what it is like. Nobody can tell you how it is or how you feel when you are homesick. You feel like you are surely going to die before you get back home.

Anyway, that's how it was that spring. I knew I couldn't play major-league ball feeling that way.

In Birmingham, Anne and I first moved into an apartment with two old people, not far from the park, and Anne did all the cooking. One night I heard her holler that the kitchen was on fire. Some French-fried potatoes she was cooking caught fire. The more water I poured on, the more it blazed up, so I threw the frying pan, potatoes, grease, and all out the window.

Then we moved into Mrs. Mauch's boarding house, where five or six of the ballplayers and their wives stayed. Mrs. Mauch was the mother-in-law of Legrant Scott, who met his wife at that same fine table they set and who later played with me on the Phillies. One of the great things about baseball is that you get to know who people are.

Anne could make a dress for about $2 in those hard times, that looked as good as anything she could buy in a store. I made up my mind then that when I started making good money I would buy her anything she wanted.

We really had a dandy ball club at Birmingham. Fresco Thompson was manager, one of the great men in the long line of great managers and understanding people I have played for. Fresco used to tell me about the time he was playing for the Phillies when they must have been as lousy a ball club as when I played for them much later. They would go into Chicago to play the Cubs, who had three pitchers—Charley Root, Guy Bush, and Pat Malone—who would throw a ball at you if you looked hard at them. Lefty O'Doul was playing for the Phillies then, and Lefty would say, "Fresco, get on those pitchers." And Fresco would really ride them. Lefty would get his two or three hits, and Fresco would get hit three times and be 0 for 1. One day, after this had been going on, Fresco heard Lefty kidding with the Cub pitchers, buttering them up, telling them how good they were. Then it dawned on Fresco that Lefty wanted the pitchers to get mad at Fresco so they would forget about old Lefty.

Fresco had his hands full when we played in New Orleans. All the fellows liked that town and would head for the French Quarter first chance. The girls in the strip shows didn't get off until four or five in the morning, and many a time there was ballplayers waiting for them. There was wide-open gambling in some of the parishes. One player decided to try his luck one night after a game, and we didn't see him for two days. He dropped $2000. Fresco fined him $100 for each game he missed and $50 for being a lousy gambler. I knew that player a long time after that and never did know him to gamble any more.

One night Fresco found out that two pitchers that roomed together had girls in their room until 3 A.M. He ordered them both to come to his room at 9 A.M. One of the pitchers said, "Now let me handle this. I will do all the talking." When they got down there he was too scared to open his mouth, so the other pitcher said, "Fresco, I will tell you how it was, but I won't do it again."

Fresco said, "I can't fine you because you are pitching good ball and will pitch every day if I want you to." Then he turned to the other pitcher and said, "You don't get anybody out and you don't pitch once a week. But if I fine you, I have to fine him." So instead of fining them, he gave them such a chewing out that neither one of them drank anything stronger than milk the rest of the year or had any girls in their room for a long time.

One club I liked to pitch and hit against in that league was Nashville, where they had just about the shortest right-field fence in baseball. I was a right-field hitter and figured I could hit at least one home run a game there. The way I could throw that ball in those days, when I wasn't too wild, I figured my home run would be enough to win for me. They gave you a case of beer for every home run you hit, so I would get the bellboy to ice up the bathtub when I left the hotel. They would send my beer up to the room as soon as I hit my home run, and it would be good and cold after the game.

That was a good league. We rode the train in that league.

3

At the Bottom of the Top

It wasn't until August of that year, 1938, that the Cubs
sent for me. I got in two games and pitched ten innings
without winning or losing. But I was in the major
leagues, to stay as long as I lasted as a major-leaguer.

All I knew at the time was that I was there, and it
was a time when the greats were there. If I never made
it another day, I could say, "I had a cup of coffee with
the big boys." I have often thought when I was down
and out that it is better to be a has-been than a never-
been-at-all. When I see fine ballplayers like Hank
Thompson sentenced for armed robbery in Texas, I
know the road he has traveled, and it makes me want
to cry.

We were playing a series in Atlanta in August when
Fresco told me to get packed and catch the night train
to join the Cubs in St. Louis. I was glad that on an

off-day coming into Atlanta I had got to go home and spend a day with my dad, who hadn't been at all well since the winter before. My dad and I were about as close as a father and son can be. We went hunting and fishing together, and I used to travel with him in his broken-glass business when I could during the winter. It was the last time I would see him alive, but I didn't realize how sick he was.

I went to the Chase Hotel in St. Louis, where the Cubs were staying, and was given a room, but I didn't know who my roommate was until after the game that day, and who walked in but Dizzy Dean. The Cubs had bought him from the Cardinals for $185,000, and he pitched good ball for them all year.

We went from St. Louis to Philadelphia, and I started the first game. I went five innings and was taken out for a pinch-hitter with the score tied 2–2. We went on to win it. I only pitched ten innings altogether that year, but Gabby Hartnett told me I helped the ball club quite a bit in its drive to the pennant by giving him a chance to rest his starting pitchers.

The Pirates were three games ahead of us when we took them on in a three-game series at home. I was in the bullpen all three games. We won the first two and were tied with them in extra innings in the third game. Darkness was closing in, and the umpires said one more inning was all we would play. In our half, Gabby took a mighty swing at where he thought the ball was coming out of the gloaming and hit it into the night to win the game and give us a tie for the lead. I always thought maybe that great home run was why they decided never to put lights in Wrigley Field.

With seven games to play, we won three straight

from the Giants and went to St. Louis for a four-game series one game ahead of the Pirates. We won on Friday and Saturday, but so did the Pirates. We could win the pennant by sweeping the final doubleheader. We won the first game, and the Pirates lost theirs, so we clinched it and went into the clubhouse to celebrate. The clubhouse boy told me I was wanted on the long-distance phone. It was my brother, saying our dad was dying.

I left right away for Chicago to get my car, and then drove to Columbia twenty hours without stopping except for gas and a cup of coffee, and got home thirty minutes after my dad had died. We had won the pennant, but my dad was dead, and it was the saddest day of my life. I didn't even get to see the World Series.

My brother had been running the broken-glass business while Dad was sick, and my mother ran it for five or six years afterward. I was just getting started in major-league baseball, and we had a rough time of it for a few years, but so did a lot of other people in those times.

My contract for the 1939 season with the Cubs was just $3000, which would just about cover tip money these days.

I reported back to Chicago in February in the middle of a big snowstorm with the temperature 3 below zero. I got off the train with just my suit on. People looked at me like I was nuts. There is no use saying I forgot my overcoat. I never had one.

Two days later we were on the train for the four-day trip to Southern California and on to Catalina Island, where a boy from South Carolina can get along just fine without an overcoat.

I must have run a thousand miles that spring, and I

pitched batting practice thirty days in a row. You were
supposed to get your arm loosened up by the trainer
every day before throwing batting practice. The first
time I went in, Andy Lotshaw, the trainer, started rub-
bing my left arm, and he rubbed it all spring. About
two days before we left the island, Gabby Hartnett
came in and said, "For God's sakes, Andy, Hig is a
right-handed pitcher."

Andy covered for both of us with a joke. "I know,
Gabby, but he thinks left-handed, and his left arm gets
sore too."

After Gabby left, Andy gave me down the country for
letting him rub my left arm all spring.

"My arm never bothers me, so it didn't need any rub-
bing anyway," I told him. "I figured you might as well
work on my left arm because I didn't want to deprive
you of a job."

The rookie infielders and outfielders had a rough time
even getting into the batting cage. The regulars would
stay in the batting cage until they had blisters on their
hands, but the rookies would get run out after five
swings. To get any extra hitting, they would have to
beg some pitcher to go out early and throw batting
practice. I used to throw forty-five minutes for them
and then another forty-five minutes when the regulars
started hitting.

I thought some of the older pitchers would help me,
but when I went to them for help and advice, they
said, "Learn the hard way like I did." If I stayed, somebody would have to go.

There were a good many movie stars there, making
publicity pictures and one thing and another—Betty
Grable, Loretta Young, Anita Louise and loads of star-

lets. Ronald Reagan and John Payne were there. All those movie people were great, and we had lots of fun.

The night before we left, they threw a dandy party for us with beer and whisky flowing. We played Bingo for cash prizes. When the big game for $500 started, it was hard to see the cards. Whoever won it had to be the one that could see the cards.

We stayed in Los Angeles and played ten exhibition games before starting east, playing every day and living on the train. It was a good life, especially the night life.

We were in Tucson three days, playing the Cleveland Indians. Several of us from both clubs went every night to a club where there was a big dice game. One night I lost $700 and then borrowed $100 from my roomie and got a hot hand and ended up winning $1400.

Oscar Vitt, managing the Indians that year, would send his catcher out with two hard-drinking pitchers to watch out for them. The catcher never did any drinking, but in the morning the pitchers would show up fresh and bright, and the catcher would look like he had been through the mill.

In Amarillo, Texas, there was a fair where several of us bought throws at a booth and won twenty big teddy bears before they run us away. There was a fellow there had spent $25 trying to win one, so I gave him one of mine. That same night there were fights every place we went. Two fellows were arguing about who would win the American League pennant, and one put on brass knucks and belted the other across the bridge of the nose. They carried him away. Next day we saw in the paper where he died.

I pitched good relief ball for the Cubs the early part of that season and was given three fine raises in five weeks. Then Gabby, who was now manager, called me into his office and said, "Hig, I hate to tell you this, but you have been traded to the Phillies for Claude Passeau. We tried to give them somebody else, but Doc Prothro wouldn't take anybody but you." The Cubs also got Ray Harrell, a pitcher, and Joe Marty, an outfielder, because Claude was an established star.

Doc was a fine manager who drank about twenty Cokes a day and was as nervous as a cat in a room full of rocking chairs. Managing that club would have made anybody nervous.

After driving two days from Chicago, I got to the ball park about 4 P.M., and Doc asked me if I could pitch that night. I said, "That's what I'm here for."

We were playing Pittsburgh, which had some power with the Waner brothers, Arky Vaughan, and Bob Elliott. I saw that night how things were going to be. I gave up five hits and got beat 1–0.

They called us the Futile Phillies. We won 44 games in 1939, but did better in 1940, when we won 45.

About the middle of the first season, old Hughie Mulcahy had won 10 and lost 9, and the sports writers were saying he could be the first pitcher to win 20 for the Phils since Grover Cleveland Alexander. He pitched great ball but ended up something like 11 and 22. I ended up 12 and 15.

One game, when Boom Boom Beck was pitching for us against Bucky Walters and the Reds, the infield booted in two runs in the first inning. Then Boom Boom didn't give them a chance to boot the game away until the thirteenth inning. After the game, he told Doc to lock the clubhouse doors, and he really gave those ballplayers hell. He said his wife could play infield better with an apron on than any of them. He said he was going to buy them all aprons and tell them when to drop the aprons to stop a ball.

How much good his talking did showed up the next day, when I went out and got beat by Paul Derringer 2–1 in twelve innings. I gave up two hits, and both runs were unearned.

We took a nine-game losing streak into the Polo Grounds for a four-day series. The Giants beat us the first two games. I pitched the first game of the Sunday doubleheader and got beat in the eleventh inning 1–0 when Harry Danning broke his bat and hit a Chinese home run that just made it down that short right-field line. That was our twelfth loss in a row. We went into the bottom of the tenth in the second game tied 2–2. They got us out in the eleventh, and Doc said, "Hig, they are going to call the game on account of darkness after this inning. For God's sakes, go in there and get us a tie."

The first man up hit a ball to our shortstop, who picked it up beautifully and nearly killed a spectator in a box behind first base with his throw. With the runner on second, I walked the next man intentionally, and they bunted the runners up. With runners on second and third and one out, I loaded the bases with another intentional walk. The next hitter lifted a short fly to our center fielder. The runner on third didn't even make a feint as if he was going to try to score after tagging up, but our center fielder threw anyway—all the way to the top of the screen behind home plate. That made it thirteen in a row for us and two losses for old Hig in one day.

In the clubhouse, old Doc said, "I want the whole

club to go out tonight and get drunk, loosen up." I don't know what he meant, because that club was never anything but loose. Doc was waiting on me when I got in about 7 A.M. "Hig, what in the world did you go out and get loaded for? I don't want you associating with that bunch of bums."

There were games when I could have whipped everybody in the stands by myself. But one Friday night Mulcahy beat Cincinnati, and the next day I beat them. Our winning streak drew the biggest crowd I ever saw in Philly, about twelve thousand fans. Doc said, "Hig, you may have to relieve in both games. We don't want to look bad in front of all these people." But we were down six runs in the first game before I could get to the bullpen, and we lost the second game 11–1. We didn't draw that many people the whole rest of the year.

The man who owned the ball club, a Mr. Baker, had died and left the club to his secretary, but he didn't leave any money to run it with. So Gerry Nugent, the husband of the secretary, sold promising players every year to stay in business. With the players he sold, you would have had one of the best all-star teams of those years. Among them were Passeau, Bucky Walters, Dolph Camilli, Chuck Klein, Curt Davis, and Dick Bartell.

When a good ballplayer went to the Phillies, he would hustle and bear down in the hope he would be sold to a good ball club. It was hard to pitch for that club, but I kept thinking I would be with a good club if I kept on trying.

Some of the ballplayers gave up trying, and then they weren't even good enough for the Phillies to unload. Some of the players had been big stars in their time. If we could have taken seven or eight years off them, we would really have had a big-league club. They had plenty of heart, but the old legs just wouldn't go.

One of the outfielders was about as strong and smart as an ox. He would go up to the plate, especially with men on base, and take three mighty swings and come back to the bench with the runners still on base. "They didn't cheat me out of my swings," he would say. One day I told him, "Anybody can go up there and knock the air out of the park. I want to see somebody go up there and hit the ball and drive in a few runs." He got real mad and wanted to fight.

We had a little catcher named Walter Millies, a good receiver but not much of a hitter. Little Walter came up to bat in the last of the ninth in a 3–3 game against St. Louis, a man on third and one out. The Cardinal outfield came in on him so it looked like seven infielders. Walter hit a tremendous clout for him, a short fly to right, but Slaughter was playing him so close it went over his head. The runner scored and won the game, but Walter sprinted to second base. The official scorer gave him credit for a double because it was the first extra-base hit of his career, and I bet he never did get another.

That was the first full year in the majors for both Mort Cooper of the Cardinals and me, and we both made the rookie team. I was pitching against him in St. Louis, going into the eighth tied 1–1, and I got the first two men out. Then Slaughter hit a line drive right at our center fielder. All he had to do was raise his glove, but he charged in under it. When we got the ball back,

Slaughter was sitting in the dugout. Old Hig had lost another one, and Mort had another win.

After one like that, the players would pat me on the back: "Tough luck, Hig." I got tired of that tough-luck stuff.

The victories were so far between that we pitchers figured we were entitled to a night out to celebrate every time we won one. We had two pitchers that had so few chances to celebrate they went the other way and drowned their sorrows when they lost.

You have to have one run before you go out to the ball park. With the Phillies you needed four or five, because on a good day our club would give away two or three. We had some pitchers that really bore down all the way, and it was heartbreaking to see them pitch really fine games and get beat because we didn't get any runs or booted the games away.

After the season I went home for a month and then back to Philly to talk contract with Mr. Nugent. My hotel and food cost me more while I was there negotiating than the raise I got. But he did promise me a bonus of $1000 if I won 15 games the next year. I had won 12, and he said we were going to have a much better club in 1940 so I ought to win 15 easy.

We went to Miami for spring training, and the rooms in our hotel were so small you had to go out in the hall to change your mind. When you shaved you dusted the mirror with your eyelashes. You had to leave a window open or you couldn't get the key in the keyhole. It was nothing like Catalina and being with a first-place club. We rode bicycles from the hotel to the ball park.

We had a good spring exhibition season for us. We

won four games. When we opened in New York, I pitched against Carl Hubbell. We were 1–1 in the seventh. Babe Young hit a ground ball to Gus Suhr at first base. When I ran over to cover the base, he said, "Hig, hold them until I come to bat again, and I'll hit a home run off old Carl and win this one for you." Damn if he didn't. We won it 3–1, but even this great event didn't get too much attention. That was the day Bob Feller pitched a no-hitter opening game against the White Sox.

It rained the next three days, and we went back for the opener in Philly. Doc said, "You pitch the opener here too, Hig. Maybe you can win them all this year if it rains enough."

Harry Gumbert of the Giants and I had a 0–0 duel going into the eighth. I had the bases loaded, with Mel Ott the hitter. I went to 3 and 2 on him and tried to get him with a curve. It went a little low and forced in the run. They beat me 1–0. I told Doc that I didn't believe I would take him up on his offer to pitch them all.

After the game my wife asked me why I didn't throw Ott a fast ball. "You might have got it over the plate." I was mad about losing anyway, and by the time I got through telling her why I threw the curve ball, she just did the cooking and didn't come out to see me pitch a game for a month.

She decided to go when I was pitching against the Dodgers. The first five men got hits off me. When she walked into the park I was already in the showers. She said to the fellow sitting next to her, "I thought Higbe was going to pitch today." He said, "The bum started and has departed." I told her next time she wanted to see me pitch, come to the park early.

I started the last game of that series against the Dodgers. Whitlow Wyatt and I were having a real good 1–1 game. Joe Medwick came up for them in the seventh and hit one out of town and laughed all the way around the bases. I didn't see anything funny about it. When he crossed home plate, I hollered, "You'll be up there again, and we'll see who gets the next laugh." He came up in the ninth, and I let him have one in the ribs. He started out after me. But Benny Warren threw the ball back to me, and I told Joe I would let him have another in the ribs. He trotted down to first. But they beat me 2–1.

In the clubhouse I really gave the ball club hell for not getting me any runs. They promised me plenty of runs next time I pitched. It was against Paul Dean and the Giants, and damn if we didn't win 19–2. They said, "See, Hig, all you gotta do is ask."

Once, after losing eight in a row, we went into New York and Mulcahy beat them 3–0. We decided we were going to celebrate the victory. One of the players started throwing soft-drink bottles out of the window of his room in the Governor Clinton Hotel. One went through the top of a taxi, and he had close misses with a dozen others before the police figured out where the bombs were coming from. They were going to lock him up until they found out he played for the Phillies. One of the cops said, "Let them have their fun. They don't have much chance to celebrate."

We lost the next seven in a row before I beat Cincinnati 3–2 in eleven innings.

When we played Boston, it was something to see each team trying to give the game back to the other. We were fighting for last place, and Boston was fight-

ing to take it away from us. We beat them out both
years.

We had one pitcher who could really throw that seed
for six or seven innings; then they would start knocking him around. After pitching seven and two-thirds
no-hit innings against the Cubs, he told Doc, "I really
pitched a good game out there for seven innings."

"Son," Doc said, "you are in the big leagues now, and
all the games up here go nine innings."

"After pitching on this club for a couple of months,"
the boy said, "I'm not sure whether I'm in the big
leagues or not."

"Don't ever think you are not in the big leagues, son,"
Doc told him. "We may not be a big-league club, but
we are playing against big-league clubs."

Old Doc was a fine manager, and he really wanted
to win, but you have got to have the horses to win, and
he didn't have them. I bet he walked ten thousand
miles in the third-base coaching box that season.

As we came to the last game of the season, I had
won 14 and lost 19. The last game was my chance to
win 15 and earn the $1000 bonus Mr. Nugent had
promised me. It was raining at Ebbets Field, but the
Dodgers wanted to get the game in to keep from giving
refunds, and I wanted my chance at number 15. We
waited and finally got started. We made five errors and
got beat 2–1. Neither run was earned. I told Mr. Nugent
I thought I deserved the bonus. He said, "You didn't
win fifteen." I didn't get it.

In November I went back to Philly to talk contract.
I talked for three days, trying to get up to $10,000. He
showed me every contract on the club, and the highest
was for $7500. He said, "Hig, I will give you eighty-five

hundred, and you will be the highest-paid man on the ball club."

If he was going to trade me or sell me to another club, I decided I would wait and bargain with the new club. So I asked him. He said, "Not a chance." I believed him and signed. I left Philly that cold night and drove home. At midnight I turned on the radio for the news and heard that I was sold to the Brooklyn Dodgers for $100,000 and three players (pitchers Vito Tamulis and Bill Crouch and catcher Mickey Livingston). I was shocked but deliriously happy. When I got home I called Mr. Nugent and asked him to pay my bonus out of the $100,000 he got for me. He said the money was all spent. But Mr. Larry MacPhail, the Dodgers' president, raised my salary to $10,000. I spent the winter hardly able to wait to go to spring training with the Dodgers.

4

Old Ernest and Case

Ernest Hemingway used to hang around with us ball-players the two springs (1941 and 1942) we trained in Cuba. He and Hugh Casey took to each other from the start, and we three became good friends. Ernest was one of the roughest, toughest, but finest fellows you would ever want to meet. I had known Hugh from the Southern League, and I knew then that he would be a great relief pitcher in the majors.

First thing after every practice Case and I would meet Hemingway and stop at a bar to have a few cold beers. Then about a dozen of us would go to the Havana Gun and Country Club to shoot doves until dark. We worked out on the ball field seven days a week, and we shot doves every day afterward. The boys that usually went shooting with old Ernest, Case, and me were Curt Davis, Billy Herman, Augie Galan, Newel

Kimball, Freddie Fitzsimmons, Johnny Allen, Whitlow Wyatt, Mickey Owen, Pee Wee Reese, and Pete Reiser.

There were about twenty traps in the center of a big arena. You would stand at the edge of the circle and call, "Pull!" and a pigeon would be released from one of the traps, but you never knew from which one. You had better damn sight kill the bird before it got over the fence or it counted against you. A bird that dropped outside the fence was a miss, and it cost you money. All the bird-shooting I did as a boy and between seasons in South Carolina saved me money, but I don't think any of us was any better than old Ernest. I don't recall he ever had to pay a single round.

We would shoot maybe 500 birds a day at 25 cents a bird, so it could get expensive to be a loser. All the birds we killed, mostly young squabs, would go to the hospital or the orphans' home.

From there we would either go to Ernest's house or to one of the night clubs, Sans Souci or Casino Nacional. They were both real nice and had floor shows, gambling, and most any kind of entertainment you could ask for. Case and Ernest and I preferred the crap tables. We would shoot for hours, sometimes win, but lose most of the time. While we were gambling, the drinks were on the house, and the way old Ernest and Case put the drinks down, the losses weren't so much.

I remember one night which was like so many nights we had together. After shooting doves, we went back to the Nacional Hotel bar. Five rum and Cokes later we took off for the Casino Nacional and played blackjack for a few hours. We had pretty good luck there, so we went to the Sans Souci and got hold of the dice. Ernest made twelve passes. He wasn't doubling up as usual or we would have ended up owning the club, but he won $600 or $700. He gave most of the money he won away. He used to say, "These are fine people down here, but they don't make much money." He would stop people in the street and give them $5 or $10 each.

We made two more clubs and then about 3 A.M. Ernest said to Case, "Let's go up to my house and put the gloves on a spell." So up into the hills we waddled and had a few more drinks. Then they put the gloves on and stood there toe to toe in the living room, belting each other. They wrecked two fine chairs and a beautiful sofa. About 4 A.M. Ernest's wife couldn't stand it any more and she broke it up. Old Case and I bade them a good night and went back to our hotel. You never saw anybody enjoy boxing like Hugh and Ernest.

Ernest weighed about 230 pounds and had a gray beard and was an outdoor type of man who really did love brutal physical contact. He and Case would put on the boxing gloves every time we went up in the hills to his house. We would have a few drinks and bat the breeze and listen to Ernest tell about the experiences he had based his books on. Then you could see them itching to put the gloves on—and I don't mean big pillow gloves. Both of them could hit like a mule kicks. Old Ernest would belt Case one, and down he would go. Case would belt old Ernest, and down he would go. They brawled all over the room for five or ten minutes, laughing all the time. They had great admiration for each other. The furniture would really take a beating.

Both were big men capable of handling rough stuff. I can't think of anyone I would rather have on my side in a rough-and-tumble street brawl than those two big rascals. I have met plenty of rough men in my life, but never any rougher than old Ernest and Case. They did love life and lived it to the hilt.

They both had hearts as big as they were. When there was a call to go out to the orphanage to talk to the children, we went. You should have seen old Ernest and Case with those kids. Ernest could speak fluent Spanish, and he and Case would have as much fun with those orphan kids as they did belting each other around the room.

One night we were sitting in a bar and got to talking about drinking. Ernest said, "I do believe that if a man can handle his whisky and not make an ass of himself that drinking is good for him." I believe he actually despised a drunk man.

All the times I saw Ernest drink quite a bit, I never could tell he had had a drink.

Case was like old Ernest that way. He would drink, but I never saw him drunk, and he didn't like to see anybody drink who couldn't handle it. When pitchers drank and he had to relieve too much, he would give them down the country and say, "Don't ask me to come in here and help you. If you can't have a few drinks and stay in shape to pitch, cut it out."

Case said, "You know, Ernest, I always pitch better when I have a few the night before. You can't win ball games on milk shakes. When I have had a few the night before, I always have a guilty feeling out there, and I bear down a little harder."

"Well, Case, old pal," Ernest said, "let's have a few more. You just might be in there tomorrow, and I want to be sure you'll start throwing with a guilty feeling."

Larry MacPhail once asked Casey, with a month to go in a tough season, if he could hold out, and Case said, "Larry, if the whisky holds out, I can make it."

Case was the greatest friend I ever had. While we were with the Dodgers, we roomed together.

He was a tough man out there on the mound. One night the Cardinals were getting to him pretty good, and the way Leo stomped out to the mound, I knew he was going to get relief for him. But he and Leo talked a while, and Leo left him in. I never saw so many batters hit the dirt as I saw after that. Case hit eight or nine. They beat us 9–1.

When we got back to the hotel, I asked him why Leo left him in. He said, "It looked like the game was lost anyway, so I asked Leo to leave me in and I would teach those hitters a lesson they would never forget. I told him I'd put Ford Frick's name on the sides and backs of those hitters." (Mr. Frick was president of the National League then, and his name was on the balls.)

If a batter hit a good foul off you in those days, you would let him know you were out there on that mound; you would turn the bill of his cap around with your next pitch.

That spring, before a doubleheader against a Cuban team, Case said, "Roomie, I'll bet you a bottle of rum I can hit more Cubans today than you can." I didn't hit but eight, and old Case got twelve that day. I don't think Hugh ever wanted to hurt anybody. He just played it a little rough. When anybody said anything to him about throwing at them, he would tell them their pitcher had the same chance at him. Nothing ever bothered Hughie.

I used to like to sit in a bar in Havana with old Ernest and Case and listen to Hemingway tell about his experiences all over the world. He told us how he was turned down for military service in the First World

War because of a bad eye. He went to all the services two or three times each, trying to get in. He was working for a newspaper then, I think the Kansas City *Star* he said it was, and it came over the wire that the Red Cross was looking for volunteers to drive ambulances. He and a friend signed up and were sent to England, then to Italy.

Getting close to the action wasn't enough for Ernest. He wanted to be in it. One trip he went all the way to a forward post and handed out chocolate bars to the Italian soldiers, and they thought he was a general. He heard something like a freight train coming in, and when he woke up two of the Italians were dead and the third was screaming. Ernest picked him up and carried him back toward an aid station under machine-gun fire. He got hit in the ankle and then the knee. He crawled the last ten yards to the aid station and learned that he had been carrying a dead man. His kneecap was blown off. He said he put his head on his knee and "my face went inside my knee." He had also been hit in the right leg. They took a hundred pieces of shrapnel out of him, and he was in the hospital three months and came out with a metal kneecap and had to walk with a cane for quite a spell after that.

He would tell us about the books he had written. He talked about *For Whom the Bell Tolls* more than any other, and he told us about the real experiences he had blowing up the bridge.

He talked about Gary Cooper a great deal and how they went big-game hunting together. I never met Gary Cooper, but I know he must have been a great fellow from the admiration Ernest had for him.

He told us about the elephants, lions, tigers, and hippos he had hunted. I don't think anything ever really scared him. He and Hughie were a great deal alike in many ways.

When old Hughie walked in from the bullpen, it would look like he was walking uphill. Leo would say something like, "Case, the tying and winning runs are on base with one out, so you have to get them out." Old roomie would say, "I can see, Skipper. I been here all day too." And he would never change his expression. In those tight situations he never showed anything except that he was going to give it everything he had. He always did.

I was in Jacksonville, playing for Montgomery, in 1952 when a sports writer called me at 4 A.M. and told me that Hugh Casey had killed himself. Case sat on the side of the bed in a hotel room in Atlanta with the barrel of a 16-gauge shotgun under his chin and pulled the trigger. People said it was because he and his wife had really called it quits.

Old Case loved his wife, I know for sure because I roomed with him for six years. I never saw him with another girl, which was unusual for ballplayers. I have come into our room many a night to find him sitting up reading a Western magazine and sipping a big water glass full of whisky.

He and his wife separated several times. Once was right before he was given his unconditional release by the Dodgers. He showed me the check for $20,000 he got for signing with the Pirates. He said, "Roomie, old Case isn't through yet. Somebody still thinks he can pitch." Shortly after that he and Kay went back together, and he was as happy as he used to be when they were together in their bar and restaurant on Flatbush Avenue.

It was always crowded. He would go around with

her, greeting people—average people, poor people, gangsters, and millionaires—wearing a big red carnation and looking like the happiest person alive. I used to say, "Roomie, let me have twenty. I want to tip the waitress." He would take out a roll of $50 and $100 bills big enough to choke a hog and say, "You sure that's enough, roomie?"

Old Ernest went out the same way as Case. A good friend of Hemingway's told me about the last time Ernest and Gary Cooper were together. They both knew that Gary was going to die of cancer. Ernest said, "Coop, you think you are in bad shape, but I am going to beat you to the barn."

I never will forget the last night old Ernest and Case and I were together in Cuba the spring of 1942. We went to Hemingway's house after shooting the doves, and Ernest and Case had a few rounds with the gloves. Then we sat there sipping a few.

Ernest was telling about some of his experiences and his writing, and Case sat looking at Ernest like a little boy looking at his hero, his eyes taking in everything about him. Then Case started telling about how he pitched different ballplayers, how he would knock them down and dare them to get up. Ernest drank it all in, the same way Case had.

We left around 1 A.M. I will always remember old Ernest and Case walking arm in arm to the door, shaking hands with those big strong hands, saying so long, see you soon, maybe in New York or on the road somewhere.

Case and I went back to our hotel and up the fire escape to our room.

Nobody but God knows how much alike Case and old Ernest were.

5

Tops with the Tops

We had a real good spring training that first year in Cuba, and we felt confident. Just before we left Havana, Leo Durocher (who I'm going to tell more about in the next chapter) got us all together and said, "Boys, we are in pretty good shape now, and we have a chance to win it all this year. Let's win it for the greatest fans in the world." From playing in Ebbets Field against the Dodgers, I already knew there were no fans like the Brooklyn fans, and I already felt a thrill like I was going home instead of to a strange Northern city.

We were going to fly to Florida and play our way north against the Yankees. We got to the airport about two hours before plane time, and Case suggested a little poker while we were waiting. There were eight of us in the game, playing for good stakes. Our money and a bottle of rum was on the table. A stranger came up and said something which we thought meant he wanted to get in the game. Case told him to wait until after this hand. The man pulled a big pistol and stuck it right in Case's belly. Hugh pushed it away, and we were all ready to jump him. Then he fished out his police badge. He was going to take us all to jail for playing poker in the airport. While Case argued with him, two or three would walk off. Then I took over, and the rest got away. Finally there was only Case and me left. "Well, roomie," Case said, "it looks like we are the losers in this game." But somebody called Batista's office, and he sent a big shot down to call off the law. We just did make the airplane.

We stayed in Florida for a week and then played exhibition games with the Yankees all the way to Brooklyn. I pitched in Baltimore, and we beat them 9–1. Their only run was a homer by George Selkirk. I walked thirteen men, but I must have had pretty good stuff in the clutch.

When we got to Brooklyn there were five thousand fans at the station to meet us. You would think we had already won the World Series instead of just coming in to start the season. Billy Herman told me that night, "Every game you play in Brooklyn is like a World Series game."

We opened that year in Ebbets Field against the Giants, and Whitlow Wyatt won for us. I pitched the second game and got beat 3–1, but the fans were all for me. We won that first series two out of three, and the Faithful started talking about beating the Yankees in the World Series.

We knew from the start the Cardinals were going to

battle us for the pennant, and they did, right down to the wire.

That was my best year. I pitched 298 innings in 48 games and won 22 and lost 9. But Whitlow Wyatt was the greatest pitcher that one year I ever saw. We say that you have to have one run before you come to the ball park. When we got Whit his one run that year, he was tough to beat. In Hughie Casey we had the best relief pitcher in baseball at the time. And we had Freddie Fitzsimmons, who was never a slouch and who had a great year. With the likes of Curt Davis, Johnny Allen, Larry French, Newel Kimball, and Luke "Hot Potato" Hamlin, we had a pretty tough pitching staff.

We had a Durocher kind of team, the kind that our fans loved and deserved. Our infield had Dolph Camilli at first, Billy Herman at second, Pee Wee Reese at short, and Cookie Lavagetto at third. Our right fielder was Dixie Walker, "The People's Cherce." In center we had a rookie, Pistol Pete Reiser, who led the league in hitting that year. In left we had one of the National League's greatest hitters, Ducky Joe Medwick. In Lew Riggs and Jimmy Wasdell we had two great pinch-hitters. Behind the plate were Mickey Owen and Babe Phelps. Leo's coaches were Charlie Dressen and Red Corrigan. And in the stands, led by Hilda Chester with her cowbell and Shorty Laurice and his Brooklyn Symphony, we had the most loyal and inspiring fans a club ever played for. Gladys Gooding played the organ and sang "The Star Spangled Banner."

If you were one of Dem Bums, you belonged to Brooklyn. At the end of the first series, I was known as Koiby Higgleby in every school and bar in Brooklyn. No place but in Brooklyn could a poor Southern boy brought up on corn bread and corn whisky learn about bagels and lox, Bar Mitzvahs and Brisses, hot pastrami and stuffed derma.

The first week I was in Brooklyn, a cop stopped me for driving the wrong way on a one-way street and demanded my license. When he saw my name, he held me on that street for forty-five minutes, talking about the Dodgers and our chances. There was a traffic jam behind us all the way to the Bridge. About a week after that Case and I were driving to the park one morning and got caught in traffic. Case signaled to a policeman and told him we were late getting to the park. He had cars backing up and pulling aside and opened a path for us in nothing flat.

There were hundreds of our fans I could still call by name: Phil and Bess Berman, Joe and Bea Meyer, the Nat Walkers; Mr. Smith, the undertaker, and his brothers; Dave Stone, the best butcher in the world; Al Greenberg and his family; Bill and Rose Burlie. I could go on naming them, all wonderful people. If I had money, I would buy a ball club and put it right in the heart of Brooklyn. No one anywhere deserves a ball club of their own like the Faithful of Flatbush.

The fans supported us every way they could. One time a fan came out of the stands after umpire George Magerkurth had called a close one against us, and had George on the ground before we could calm him down.

Another time Leo was giving Mage down the country for a call at third. And Mage was giving it right back to Leo. Mage chewed tobacco, and the juice would come spraying out a space between his front teeth when he gave Leo a blast. So Skip spat back at Mage, who said, "You can't spit on me and get away with it."

Leo said, "What do you think this is on my face and shirt, snow?" But Mage ordered him out of the game, and Skip was fined $50. The fans collected 5000 pennies and gave them to Leo to pay off his fine. Leo took them in sacks to home plate the next day, but the umpire rejected them and made him come up with the long green.

The fans were behind all of us, but I guess the player they loved best in those days was Dixie Walker. When Dixie went into a slump, the whole town rallied around him.

Our fans followed us wherever they could. There would be Dodger fans wherever we went to spring training. Often when we were playing in Boston and Philadelphia, there were more Dodger fans than home-team fans. In 1941, battling for the pennant, we clinched the championship in Boston. Watching and listening to the celebration in the stands, you would have thought Boston had just won the pennant.

In the Polo Grounds there always seemed to be as many Dodger fans as Giant fans, or more. There were more fights at our games there than in all the boxing arenas in the country. After every pitch we would peek out of the dugout to see where the next fight was breaking out. There was no compatibility between the Dodger fans and the Giant fans. One Dodger fan shot a Giant fan dead in a bar for saying something against his Bums.

There was some talk about us playing the 1941 World Series in the Polo Grounds for the sake of the extra twenty thousand tickets that could be sold. But the fans of Brooklyn would rather have not seen the World Series than see their team play it in the Polo

Grounds. It cost the players money, but we were all happy with the decision to play in Ebbets Field.

The night we got back to Brooklyn from Boston after winning the pennant, there were more people at Grand Central Station to meet us than they drew in a busy week at the Philadelphia ball park. Most of us stayed around the station with the fans all night long and enjoyed every minute of it. It was a case of mutual adulation.

After one of the World Series games that year, I was walking down a street and was hailed and invited to a Jewish wedding celebration. There was enough food of many kinds for any kind of an army, and every kind of liquor. I think that party was still going on after the World Series was over.

We split the first two games with the Yankees at the Stadium, and they beat us the first game in Brooklyn. I started the fourth game and didn't last but three and two-thirds innings. They had us 3–2 when Case came in to relieve in the fifth inning. As I recall, we scored two in the bottom of the fifth to go into the top of the ninth ahead 4–3. There were two outs and nobody on when Casey struck out Tommy Henrich for what should have been the third out and the Series squared at two games each. But the third strike got by Mickey Owen, and Tommy was safe at first base. With that life, the Yankees went on to win 7–4.

Mickey stayed in the clubhouse for two hours after the game. When he left, there were five thousand fans waiting for him outside the ballpark. They gave him the greatest ovation I ever heard. It gave us big fat goose-pimples. He got more than two thousand telegrams the next day. He said, "If it hadn't been for the Brooklyn fans, I don't think I ever could have got over that passed ball."

I have been booed in Brooklyn. I won eight in a row in one stretch in 1946 and was going after my ninth when I got knocked out in the third inning. The fans gave it to me pretty good, but I would rather have those Brooklyn fans boo me than have some fans clap and cheer. It was all right for them to criticize one of their Bums.

I hate to think of apartment buildings standing where once so many great fans came to charge the air with their excitement. They used to come early and cheer every long drive in batting practice and every snappy pick-up in infield practice, and, as Billy said, they made every game seem like the World Series.

We may not have been the greatest team in baseball, but our fans had us believing we were. Every member of the team put out his best effort for them.

It hurts me to think that Brooklyn is no longer represented by a major-league baseball team. Then again, who am I? I'm just a guy who had many thrills and has many memories as one of Dem Bums.

Hell, the name Los Angeles Dodgers doesn't even sound right.

6

Durocher

I played for Leo for close to ten years. In my book he is the greatest manager I ever heard of, met, or played for. His famous remark about nice guys finishing last wasn't meant the way some people make it sound. He was in favor of nice guys—off the field.

I felt the same way about winning and losing that I think Leo felt. I have seen players go out on a field and get their brains beat out and then run to shake the hand of the players that had beat them. Leo used to say, "Buy a steak for a player on another club after the game, but don't even speak to him on the field." He would say, "Get out there and beat them to death." Once he said, "If my mother were playing second base on the opposing team and I was on first base and the ball was hit to shortstop, I would cut her legs out from under her to break up the double play."

You show me a good loser, and I'll show you a man that loses. I have never seen a man that was much of a player that was a good loser. None of the great players were good losers. Musial, Williams, Billy Herman, Warren Spahn, Johnny Mize, Joe Medwick, Dixie Walker, Joe DiMaggio—players of that caliber were all nice fellows off the field, but all of them were fierce competitors and none of them was a good loser on the field.

Leo wanted players of hustle and desire that wanted to win. He would go to the front for that type of player. I have heard Leo chew ballplayers out for mental errors, lack of hustle, or breaking training rules, but never one time did I hear him say anything to a player for a physical or mechanical error.

I mentioned that I got beat by the Giants 3–1 in the first game I ever pitched for the Dodgers. Pee Wee Reese made two errors that let in the three runs. After the game Leo said, "Hig, you keep pitching like you did today, and you'll win twenty games. Reese is the best shortstop in the league. He'll save a lot of them for you." Pee Wee did, too.

One way you could get in trouble with Leo was not following instructions. In 1942 Bobo Newsom was going to pitch for us against Pittsburgh, and we had a meeting to go over their line-up. When we got to Vince DiMaggio, Leo said, "Bobo, I want you to pitch him a foot inside." In the seventh Vince hit a double and beat us. In the clubhouse Leo asked, "Where did you pitch him, Bobo?"

"Inside."

"How far inside?"

"About four inches."

"I told you a foot inside."

"Four inches is good enough for me," Bobo said.

I never heard so much commotion in a clubhouse.

Before one game Rex Barney started in Pittsburgh in 1946, Leo said, "Rex, I don't care how many you walk, but don't let up to get the ball over. When I think you have gone as far as you can, I will come and get you."

Rex, who could throw harder and wilder than any pitcher I ever saw, walked the first three hitters, and Ralph Kiner was next. Rex let up and got it right down the middle. Ralphie hit it over the University of Pittsburgh. Leo started for the mound. Rex left for the clubhouse. After the game Leo said, "It's a good thing you didn't stay on that mound, Rex, I would have broke you in two."

Nearly the same thing happened in a game Hank Behrman was pitching against Cincinnati when we had a one-run lead. They got runners on second and third with one out. Leo signaled to put the next man on. Hank threw one ball but got too close on the second pitch, and the batter hit a double. Leo charged the mound, but Hank was gone before he got there. Hank was lucky because we won the game. Leo said, "I should fine you five hundred. If it ever happens again, I'll guarantee you won't need the money."

Leo was right. When the boss tells you how to pitch a man, that's the way you pitch him. When you go over the line-up before a game and decide how you are going to pitch the hitters, that is the way you must pitch them, because your defense is playing them that way. I have seen second basemen playing directly behind the base catch line drives and outfielders catch balls that were ticketed for extra bases. Lucky pitcher?

No, just pitching the way he said he would in the club-house.

Leo had a way of making an opposing ball club so mad that it would beat itself. When we won the pennant in 1941, we were in a dogfight with St. Louis all the way, a game ahead or half a game behind. Every game was a big one.

In 1942 in Chicago I was pitching against Hi Bithorn and was leading 5–0 going into the sixth. Hi, who could really throw that pea, knocked down Dolph Camilli and Billy Herman and got us out in the top of the sixth. I hung a curve on the first man up against me, Lou Novikoff, and he hit it a country mile. The next hitter was Jimmy Foxx. The change of pace I threw him didn't miss my head by an inch and sounded like a bunch of bees going by. It went into the center-field seats for another home run.

Leo came out to the mound and said, "Hig, don't let them take the bread and butter out of your mouth." I knew what he meant. The next hitter was Big Bill "Swish" Nicholson, who had sawdust dripping off the end of his bat, he had that much power. I flattened him four times. I flattened the next hitter four times. I got them out without further scoring and was leading 5–2 going into the seventh.

Jimmy Wilson, the Cubs manager, brought a fast-baller named Erickson in to pitch. He knocked Mickey Owen down four times. When I went to the plate, somebody on the Cubs bench yelled, "Knock him down a few times." I hollered back, "He ain't got the guts."

The first two pitches were between my head and my cap. When I squared around to bunt down the first-base line so I could walk up his back as he came over to field it, he knocked me down two more times. Reese, our lead-off hitter then, went down four times. So the bases were loaded for Billy Herman. Damn if Erickson didn't knock him down three times. Billy looked to Leo, and Leo gave him the hit sign. Billy hit the next pitch clean out of the ball park.

When I went out to pitch the bottom of the seventh, I was as mad as I have ever been. Leo walked to the foul line with me. "Hig, I have got what I wanted done. If you throw at anybody else, it is going to cost you five hundred dollars." The Cubs were expecting me to throw at them, but I didn't, and they didn't get another hit. We won 9–2. They gave us four runs, which is what Skipper wanted. He had our whole club feeling and playing to win.

Whichever way Leo went in a game, he went to win. Whitlow Wyatt was pitching for us against Mort Cooper in St. Louis, and we took a 1–0 lead into the bottom of the ninth. The first man up singled, and Slaughter doubled. Leo went to the mound but came right back, leaving Whit in to pitch to Terry Moore, Johnny Mize, and Stan Musial. (Damn! Wasn't that a line-up!) Whit struck out Moore and Mize, and Musial popped out.

One of us asked Leo what he said to Whit. "I didn't say anything to him. He told me, 'I'll get 'em, Skip. I haven't pitched all day for nothing.' So I left him in."

He came out to me in the ninth inning at Boston. I had had them shut out 5–0, but now they had two runs in, two men on, and big Ernie Lombardi coming up to hit, tough up at that plate. If he had had speed, he would have had a .400 lifetime average. Leo said, "Hig, how do you feel?"

I said, "Great, Skipper."

"A home run will tie it up."

"What do you want me to throw him, Skip?"

He said, "Throw him an out ball." And walked back to the bench.

I threw him three fast balls and struck him out. In the dugout Leo asked, "What did you throw him, Hig?"

I said, "I threw him that out ball you called for."

Another time I was pitching a two-hitter at home against Chicago, 0–0 as we came in to hit in the bottom of the ninth. The first man popped up, then Mickey Owen tripled, and I was next. The fans wanted me to stay in and hit and hold them in the tenth if we couldn't get the run home. But Leo took me out and put himself in as the pinch-hitter. Then he put the sign on for a squeeze bunt. He laid it down perfect, and it was our game. Vern Olsen, pitching for the Cubs, picked the ball up and threw it over the back of the grandstand.

Leo put himself on the spot, but it was no fluke that he came through. That spring in Cuba, Leo had us practicing bunts. The failure to lay down a decent bunt has cost more ball games than almost any ballplayer will admit. Several of us weren't doing too good in this session, so Leo took a bat and went in there to show us how. He laid down seven or eight perfect bunts. Billy Herman piped up and said, "You should be able to bunt, Skip. That's all you did for about ten years." Leo gave us extra work that day. Billy should have kept his mouth shut.

The only time in my career I ever disagreed with Leo was in another ninth-inning situation in 1946, when we were leading Cincinnati 2–1 at home, me against Bucky Walters. With a man on first and two outs, I was working on the last man. He hit a ball up in the air so high I got to the bench thinking I was the winner. Eddie Stanky and Dixie Walker each thought the other had the ball, and it dropped in for a double. So I had to go back and pitch. Leo had me walk a man to load the bases, and the next hitter broke his bat and got a base hit and beat me 3–2. I came in, and Leo said, "Hig, you wasn't trying." I was mad, but I saw he was so mad he didn't know what he was saying. He knew that old Hig gave him all he had all the time.

The day before the Kentucky Derby in 1941 I was going out to pitch against Cincinnati, and Leo said, "Hig, if you win today, I will let you off to see the Derby tomorrow." I got beat 1–0, but I went to him and said, "Skip, I pitched a good game and think you ought to let me off to go to the Derby."

He said, "Not good enough. If you had wanted to go to the Derby bad enough, you would have pitched a shut-out and hit a home run." He meant win, not just come close to winning.

Leo never doubted his confidence. One time Johnny Allen was pitching against Cincinnati in their ball park, a 0–0 game. In the fifth Leo said, "Hold them right there, Johnny, we'll get you a run." Every inning he kept promising Johnny a run until the twelfth, when Johnny said, "Skip, you're kidding me about that run, aren't you?" Johnny pitched fifteen innings before Leo sent Case in to relieve. We went into the nineteenth, still 0–0, and it was getting dark. We scored five runs in our half, and Bill McKechnie, the Reds manager, started stalling in his half, hoping to get the game called on account of darkness. Umpire Larry Goetz told him we were going to finish the game if the players had to wear miners' hats with lights. Leo told old Hugh, "Case, just get the ball over. We will get them out for you." But they got two men in and had two on with one out. Then Frank McCormick nailed one on the nose, but right at Pee Wee, who caught it and stepped on second for the double play. Pee Wee said he never saw the ball; it just happened to hit his glove and stick. Leo said to Case, "I told you we'd get 'em out for you." In the clubhouse he said to Allen, "Johnny, I told you we'd get a run for you if you just hung in there."

Leo was competitive about everything he did and, like all winners, was capable of complete concentration. He was the best pool-player and card-player in organized baseball. He was real rough to beat.

But all the time I played for him I never saw Leo drink so much as a beer. Maybe that's why he was always on us who did.

One morning I strolled into the hotel lobby in Pittsburgh about 4 A.M., and Leo and two coaches were checking the traffic. He gave me a short speech, and "we" agreed to meet early at the park, him on one end of the fungo and me on the other, shagging fly balls.

He ran me so much that day that Johnny Allen said, "Hig, the skipper had you running like a policeman was after you." Finally Leo said, "I believe you have all the juice out of you now." By that time I must have blowed all the air out of the park too.

He used to check us in our rooms about once a week. One time (I was rooming with Newel Kimball then) I answered the phone.

Leo said, "This is Skip."

"What do you want?" I said. "You just woke your ace pitcher up who is trying to get some rest."

"I'm just checking. Where is Kimball?"

"In bed," I said and hung up.

About five minutes later he called again. I said, "Skip, Kimball and I are trying to sleep." As it happened, that was the situation.

A few minutes later there was a knock on the door. It was Senator John Griffin, the clubhouse boy.

"What do you want?"

He looked in and saw us both there. "Just checking."

The next day Leo called a meeting. "Well, boys," he said, "I hope you had a good time last night. There was nineteen of you that came in late. However, one of the guys that I was pretty sure was going to be out late last night never left the hotel. I can't fine the whole team, so let's go out and win some more."

After we won something like nine out of our next ten, I said to Leo, "I got a night coming now."

He said, "Okay, you got a night coming, and after your night, I got a day coming with my fungo." When I took a night after that, I didn't let Skip know it. That next day with the fungo was a killer.

Leo had warned one of our guys several times about drinking and having girls up to his room. One night late there were a couple of club officials in our hotel in Brooklyn when he came in with a girl on one arm and a quart under the other. They called Leo, and Leo went to his room.

The girl came to the door and said, "What can I do for you, baldy?"

"Who are you?"

"I am Madame de Fifi. Who are you?"

Leo didn't have any secrets from his ballplayers when he had to discipline one of us. Next day he called this player to the front of the meeting. He told us the story and then said to the player, "Madame de Fifi has cost you a thousand dollars and a trip to the Phillies." Skip traded him away to the salt mines.

One of our guys figured that if women and liquor were bad for Leo's players, they must be bad for the opposition. Toward the end of the 1942 season, when the Cardinals were closing in on us, this guy got a chorus girl and sent her to Philadelphia, where the Cardinals were playing while we were battling Cincinnati in Brooklyn. There was hardly no way the Phillies could beat the Cardinals, especially when one of their aces was pitching. So this girl was told to get a date with one of the Cardinal pitchers the night before he was going to pitch, and she did. Next day he shut the Phillies out on two hits.

When the girl came back, she was told she had done a lousy job.

"A lousy job! He drank two quarts of liquor, and I guarantee he didn't sleep a wink all night."

The Cardinals were coming to Brooklyn next, and the girl was given another chance.

The pitcher was due to pitch the second game, and she made a date with him. She called in the morning and said she had been with him all night and she was dead tired and didn't see how he could be good for anything that day. But he held us to a lousy three hits and beat us 2–0.

That looked like pretty good medicine for a pitcher, and I asked why they didn't try it out on me.

We had better luck winning ball games by stealing the other club's signs. We had a few hitters who didn't do anything but hang out line drives if they knew what was coming. Under Durocher, we could get the signs of all the clubs except the Cardinals and the Boston Braves. The Braves didn't use them. When Casey Stengel, then the manager, wanted a man to bunt, he would holler, "Bunt." And he would holler for the hit-and-run and take, too. Leo asked Stengel if he had any signs. "No," Casey said. "If I did, the only players who would get them anyway would be your team."

Leo and Larry MacPhail were quite a pair, real fighters both of them, and there was bound to be sparks between them. In Philadelphia in 1941 MacPhail came down to the clubhouse and told Leo to pitch Luke Hamlin. The Phils scored four runs in the first inning and beat us. Leo did not let Larry in the clubhouse the rest of the year. "If you want to see me, I will come up to your office. I'll run the ball club down here."

Right after we won the pennant in Boston that year, we were coming back victorious and celebrating on the diner. Larry sent word to have Leo stop the train at the 125th Street Station in New York so he could come into Grand Central Station with the team. Either Leo didn't get the word or he decided the diner was the clubhouse; the train didn't stop. Larry was so mad he fired him that night and hired him back the next morning.

7

The Home Front

As losers, our share of the 1941 World Series was $4850.50 each. The Yankees got about $5600 each. (That's about half of what the split is now, but our dollars were bigger.)

I went back to Columbia and looked around for a job, as I always did. People told me what they always did. "Hig, by the time you learn the job you'll be gone off playing ball again." I reckon what they weren't saying was, "Hig, you just don't have the education to hold down any good job but playing ball."

I wasn't doing too bad. MacPhail raised my pay to $12,500 for the 1942 season, which was twice what a top-paid sports writer was making in those days, and I had my World Series winnings. I invested most of that in golf. I played good golf then, par or just above or just below. Afternoons that winter, I played golf with other good players for good stakes. One of the guys I played with was a Columbia pro named Johnny Spence, who later traveled with Billy Graham and wrote a book called *A Golf Pro for God*. He was a golf pro for himself that year.

I did make a down payment of $2000 on a house, which my wife and I moved into, but otherwise my money went for golf. During my baseball career the only investments I made were speculative investments in Colorado mines, and none of them ever panned out.

The news of Pearl Harbor came, and nobody knew what was going to happen to himself or the country or the world. I figured I would be in it when the time came, and I didn't worry about it.

When spring came, I found I just didn't want to go to Cuba for spring training. The real reason was the food. I just didn't like the food there. You would order ham and eggs for breakfast, and they would bring you eggs swimming in milk. I just wasn't brought up to eat that kind of food.

I stayed in Miami for about ten days, working out with a college team. I told Leo I would get in shape there. MacPhail called me and gave me down the country about not reporting. I told him about the food, and he said I was getting to be a prima donna. "Don't forget," he said, "I took you out of the salt mines."

"Don't forget," I told him, "I pitched you to a pennant."

"Hig," he said before he hung up, "it will cost you one hundred dollars for every day you miss."

After about $1000 worth, I decided I had better get over to Cuba. First day, Leo said, "Well, Hig, did you get in pretty good shape with the college team?" He got the fungo and hit ground balls, running me from first to third. After about ten minutes I gave up. Skip said, "Hig, old boy, you're not in shape." It wasn't long before he had me in shape.

One thing, they improved the food. It wasn't only me, a lot of players didn't like it. They made a real effort, and the rest of that spring we had pretty good American food.

Old Ernest and Case and I picked up where we had left it the year before, shooting doves and drinking and talking, but that was the year MacPhail had private detectives following all the ballplayers. Hughie and I would often have to go back to the hotel and drink our rum in our room.

When we went to the airport to fly to Miami, we had to go through customs. John McDonald, our traveling secretary, had all the reports from the private detectives in his bag. The reports used numbers, not names. When the customs man read the reports of what all these numbers had been doing in Havana, they were certain they had uncovered and cornered the biggest spy ring in history. They called the FBI in on the case, and old McDonald was a long time talking our way onto the airplane.

In Miami, Leo called a meeting. "Boys," he said, "I have the evidence right here in front of me. You all know your numbers so you will know who the detectives are talking about." It took him two hours to read the whole report, but nobody was bored. It would go like this: "Numbers ten, twenty-two, and sixteen left the ball park and went to a bar and had several rum and Cokes. They returned to the hotel, had dinner, and went to a house of prostitution at two-fifty-eight

Y Street, and left there at four A.M. and went back to the hotel." It turned out that some of the ballplayers were there so much they had their laundry sent out from 258 Y Street. He got to my number, thirteen, and Hughie's, twelve, and said, "Numbers thirteen and twelve stopped at a bar after leaving the ball park and went to their room and did not leave the hotel all night." Actually Numbers 13 and 12 went out the window and down the fire escape and came back the same way. When he finished the report, Leo put heavy fines on several of the players, but to Case and me he said, "You boys have been pretty good this spring." I think he knew better.

A few nights later, while we were still in Florida, Leo came into the lobby about 11 P.M. and asked several of us hanging around to go up to a certain player's room and greet him as he came in. He got the key, and five of us went with him. Leo said we could be expecting him to come in through the window at 1:30 A.M. The player was about fifteen minutes late. He stuck his head in through the window off the fire escape and saw Leo. "Good morning, Skipper," he said, like they were meeting for breakfast. Of the many things that Leo had to say to him, the worst was $500. Some of us thought it would have been cheaper if he had stayed out all night.

There was talk that year about canceling professional baseball so that it wouldn't interfere with the war effort, but the higher-ups made the decision that baseball was good for the morale of both the working people and the fighting people.

Only a few of the ballplayers went into military service that year. We had another good ball club, but we didn't get much help from the rest of the league.

When August came, we were leading the Cards by nine games. We beat the Phillies to go ahead by 9½, and damn if MacPhail didn't call a meeting after the game to warn us that if we didn't bear down all the way the Cards just might beat us out of the pennant. It was a big joke to us.

But the Cards kept inching up and caught us and went ahead by 1½ games. Leo called a meeting and made a fighting speech. He called on us to win 7 of our last 8 games and be champions again. We did better than that. We won our last 8 games, but the Cards still picked up ½ game on us and won by 2. They won their last 9 games. We won 104 and lost 50, good enough to win the pennant any year but that one. The Cards were 106–48.

I was in 38 games that year, pitched 222 innings, and won 16 and lost 11.

The next spring, travel was curtailed for the duration, and we went to Bear Mountain, New York, for training. We worked out in the gigantic fieldhouse at West Point. We had batting practice at one end of the fieldhouse, and Army had spring football practice at the other. We would do our running outdoors, along the Hudson River, which was still covered with ice. I caught cold in my arm after throwing batting practice inside and running outside by the river. That was the only year I ever had trouble with my arm.

A man named Martin ran the Bear Mountain Inn, where we stayed, and he couldn't do enough for the Dodgers. There was a great big front room with a huge fireplace in it where they burned logs about five feet long. It was real cold up there at night, snow all over the mountains.

Some evenings we would eat with the cadets. All the freshmen ate sitting at attention. They would get their glasses from the cadet at the head of the table. He would tap one on the table and throw it down the line. The cadet that the glass was intended for had better be awake. The whole time I was at West Point, I never did see a cadet make an error.

When we started the 1943 season we already had several men in the military. Both Pee Wee Reese and Hugh Casey were in the Navy. We didn't have near the ball club we did in 1941 and 1942. I had won 6 and lost 10 when my arm finally came around, the middle of July. I won my last 7 in a row and finished up 13–10, pitching 185 innings in 35 games. We finished third.

After the season I went into the Army, along with several others. Leo wanted to go, but they turned him down. It was pretty rough on old Skipper. If he had gone in, I have a feeling that the war would have been over much sooner. He would have found some way to beat the enemy.

8

A Rifleman

On off-days during the 1943 season I used to go out to
Mitchel Field and play in exhibition games and help
with their ball club. The officers there wanted me to
come into the Air Force when I got drafted, and they
gave me papers to fill out.

In September I went through the induction center at
Fort Jackson, which was just two miles from my front
doorstep. The general told me that if I took the Army
instead of the Air Force he would keep me in Columbia
for the duration. It sounded like a good deal to me.

It was supposed to take three days to go through the
induction center, but I was pushed through in three
hours. It seemed they had a ball game to play the afternoon of the day I was inducted, so the general gave
orders that I was to be given all my examinations, shot

in both arms, and sworn in by 1 P.M. I pitched that afternoon.

I was assigned to the post MPs, but my job was baseball while the season lasted, and then the general made me manager of the basketball teams. We went to Chattanooga for the regional basketball tournament.

In my spare time I stood guard duty. On the night shift, from midnight until 8 A.M., I got in some good practice with the .45 pistol, shooting at rabbits.

In the spring we started baseball early and had a really fine team, and beat everybody in sight. In fact, nobody scored on us in nine games. So we took on Atlanta in the Southern League in a five-game series. We beat them at Fort Jackson 3–0 and 11–0, and then we went to Atlanta for three games, traveling in staff cars and staying at a nice hotel. I pitched and won on Friday and beat them 7–0. That made twelve games we had won without being scored on. We were too good for our own good.

That night we were eating dinner with the general in a private dining room when the phone rang. I did not like the way it sounded. I said, "Sir, that sounds like trouble." It was. It was the War Department in Washington, telling the general to ship me, another player, and a little left-handed pitcher out of Fort Jackson immediately. We had given them what they wanted, a winning team, but the publicity killed the deal. The general did his best to keep me. He transferred me to headquarters company of a tank outfit. It is on my record that I was with this tank outfit, but I never saw it or it me. In a week I was on my way to Camp Butner, a repple depple (replacement depot) near Durham, North Carolina.

I reported to a major on a Friday. Damn if he didn't say, "Hig, we've got a pretty good ball club here and are playing a club tomorrow that we want to beat real bad."

I said, "I'm ready, but I don't know if I will be here that long, the way the Army is after me to be a soldier."

I pitched the next day, and we won, 3–1. There was a celebration dance that night, but I didn't have anything to wear but a baseball uniform or fatigues. They said, "You won for us today, wear anything." So I went in my fatigues and really had a ball.

On Monday the major called me in and said, "Hig, you are on orders to go to the Eighty-sixth Division at Camp Livingston, Louisiana. I have never seen a private get moved around so fast." I left that afternoon.

My orders said to report to the commanding general, 86th Division, so that is what I did. I went straight to the general's office and said, "Old Hig is here. When is the first ball game?"

He said, "If we wanted you to play ball, we would pay you what you were making in the major leagues. But we are going to make a soldier out of you." I started basic training the next day.

The first week we were crawling on our bellies under machine-gun fire. One boy saw a rattlesnake, jumped up, and got killed right quick. Old Hig made up his mind that if he saw a snake he was going to say, "Move over, big boy, there is plenty of room down here for both of us."

We knew they were getting us ready for combat. We got plenty of twenty-five-mile hikes and nine-mile forced marches.

Even then I didn't get entirely away from baseball.

The post had a pretty good ball club, and the colonel wanted me to pitch for it, but I had to do it along with my basic training. Sometimes I would get up at 3:30 A.M., pull KP, take a twenty-five-mile hike, get back at 1 P.M., pitch a ball game, and go right back on KP.

I was the only one from the 86th Division asked to go to Wichita to play in the baseball tournament there, and I had to use my furlough time to go.

When I got back we were shipped to California, and we all figured we were going to fight the Japs. But after a month we were shipped back across the country to Boston. We got there about 3 A.M. in a heavy snowstorm and marched eight miles to camp. Our orders were no phone calls, no telegrams, no nothing, and three days later we were on the boat for Eruope.

We were in a huge slow convoy that took twenty-five days to cross. The last day out from Le Havre, we were alerted that German subs were close by, and we were surrounded by our destroyers dropping depth charges that shook our boat like a leaf in a storm. We made it on in. The docks at Le Havre were all blasted and torn up and looked like somebody had been mad at those people there.

We went straight to Camp Lucky Strike to get ready for combat. My outfit was the 342nd Infantry, commanded by Colonel Heffner, and my company was commanded by Captain Briscoe. After a week getting our equipment ready, we loaded into forty-and-eight railroad cars and chugged off to Germany. Those cars were supposed to carry forty men and eight horses, but with forty men in there you couldn't lie down, stand up, or fall down. I ate something out of a can that made me sick. When we stopped in some little burg, I jumped out of that car and started across a field, really sick. One of the fellows hollered to watch out for land mines, but the way I felt I knew that I wouldn't be lucky enough to step on one.

We got to Cologne, with the Germans across the Rhine River, and we crossed the next day and went into combat. I was so scared for about a week, I didn't know where I was. Anybody who wasn't scared was crazy. A platoon leader that is not afraid will get you killed. After that first week, after seeing all those bodies, I said to myself, "Hig, you are just like a dog. You will either get killed or you won't, so don't worry about it." You had to look at it that way or you would go crazy. Some of the boys did lose their minds. I have seen them refuse to go on patrols, they were that scared. They couldn't help themselves. I really felt sorry for them because I was damn near that scared myself.

The Germans were supposed to be pretty strong in our sector. So our outfit sent out patrols to probe for the enemy and find out just where they were and how strong. I was on the first patrol Captain Briscoe picked. We were lucky to have a sergeant for patrol leader who was real good and knew what he was doing, Sergeant Gardner.

We left at 10 P.M. and headed straight for where the Germans might be. We were under orders not to fire our guns unless absolutely necessary, because we were strictly after information. We went along about fifteen to twenty-five yards apart, so the enemy would have a hell of a time spotting more than one or two of us at a time. After about an hour we began spotting a few Germans. Then we saw about a company of them. We kept going, under cover as best we could, until we came upon a hell of a group of them. I came so close to some of them I could hear them breathing. After we had been gone about three hours, Sergeant Gardner gave us the sign to start back. I was always glad to get that old go-home sign. We got back with our information without being seen or firing a shot.

In fact, all the patrols I was ever on, I was never seen. We had many patrols from our outfit that were really shot up, but we were very fortunate on ours, I think because we had a great patrol leader. Sergeant Gardner weighed about 230 pounds and was 6 feet 3 and moved through the woods like an old Indian. Those patrols were a long ways from a Sunday picnic. I never did go on one without thinking sure as hell the enemy could hear my heart beating.

Another rough job was going into a town and taking it after it had been bombed and shelled for a few days. First they would bomb it, then blast it with artillery, then rake it with mortar fire. Then we would go into town and take it and secure it. There wouldn't be many buildings left standing, and the rubble made good cover for snipers. And let me tell you I didn't like those snipers one damn bit. I have had boys shot on both sides of me. And it wasn't only snipers. The Germans would pull about five miles out of a town and then shell hell out of you with those 88s when you went in to take it. I didn't have any love for those things either. Damn if they couldn't shoot those 88s like you would a rifle. When I saw one knocked out, I would always say a little prayer of thanks.

After we secured a town, the trading would start. We would be so tired of C and K rations that a fresh

egg was as great as a seven-course dinner back home.
We would scrounge around and start bartering the cigarettes and candy we got with our rations for something
different to eat and, of course, for wine and beer. We
could go to the wineries in a town and get all kinds of
wine, but beer was pretty scarce. We would get all we
could for our cigarettes and candy, because we didn't
know how long it would be before we could do some
more scrounging in another town.

We got to a little town on the banks of the Danube,
which we were going to cross at 5 A.M. We were throwing 4.2 mortars across at them, and they were letting us
have those 88s and everything else they had. You
couldn't hardly tell from the sound what we were sending and what we were receiving. During our barrage I
went into a basement to get a little more protection.
There was a German girl with her baby by a little window. I took the baby and pushed her away from the window. She started hollering and screaming. I couldn't
understand her, but the captain began to laugh. "Hig,"
he said, "she thought you were trying to rape her." You
couldn't blame those people. Whenever we took a town
in that area, the jail would be full of Russian prisoners,
and we would turn them loose. They raped a lot of
women. They said the Germans had raped and killed
their wives and sisters on the Eastern front early in the
war, now it was their turn.

The Germans blew up the bridge our engineers built
across the Danube five times. They would blow a section of pontoons out, and our boys would fix it back and
then have another section to fix. We finally went across
in rubber boats. The Germans made a direct hit with an
88 on the boat just ahead of mine and blew it all to

pieces and one of my best friends with it. I didn't see anything blue about the Danube. It was the dirtiest, muddiest water I ever saw.

In the last town we took before the war was over, there was a military headquarters. We blew the door off a big safe and found it stacked with German marks. I put quite a bit in my knapsack and used the bills to light cigarettes. When I was down to 100 marks, I found out the money was still good. Old Hig's luck was still holding. If I had bought United States Savings Bonds, the Germans and the Japs would have won the war.

But that's not right. I have always had good luck. The only bad luck I have had, I have brought on myself.

When the war was over we had fought all the way to Berndorff, Austria. That was beautiful country, snow-capped mountains and mirror lake, right across the Swiss border. Hitler's retreat was on a beautiful lake about five miles from where we were staying.

We didn't get much time to enjoy the scenery or make friends with the girls. In about a week, while the rumors were flying that we were going home, going to Japan, going to stay there as security force, etc., we were going back to Camp Lucky Strike.

A lieutenant with a jeep said, "Hig, we are not going to get this close to Paris without giving it a look." It was a hundred miles out of our way, but away we went. We stayed in Paris three days. Everywhere you would hear the proposition "Sleep with me for a pack of cigarettes." What tickled me was the toilets on the main streets. A man taking a leak would tip his hat to all the ladies passing by.

We were in Camp Lucky Strike only about ten days

before we were on the boat going home. I had a pretty good accordion and a duffel bag full of guns. I sold the guns and was broke in two days. You never saw such gambling. I wanted to get back in the game, so I sold the accordion, which must have been worth $200, for $25. There weren't too many accordion-lovers on that boat. I went in partners with a buddy and ran up our $50 to $1500. He took his $750, and I stayed in. We played continuously, and I got as high as $5000. When we got off in New York, after nine days, I had $250 left.

That old Statue of Liberty never looked better to anyone than it did to us.

We went right to Camp Kilmer in New Jersey and could have anything we wanted to eat. Steak for breakfast if we wanted it, and we did. And milk, we must have drunk a gallon each and every meal. We really did some eating.

They gave us thirty days' leave before joining up with the outfit again in Camp Gruber, Oklahoma. I stayed around Columbia a few days and went up to Brooklyn and had a few cold beers with old friends, but it wasn't the same with so many ballplayers still away. I was kind of restless anyway and went back home until time to rejoin the outfit.

They didn't mess around with the old Black Hawk Division. Two weeks later we were in a camp not far from San Francisco, waiting to ship out to the Pacific. Three of us decided we needed one last fling, so we went over the fence and into San Francisco and got a room at the Mark Hopkins, first class. We had a Friday, Saturday, and Sunday of living it up and got back Monday, just as our outfit was leaving for the boat. They gave us hell and said they were going to court-martial us, but we didn't have much luck. While the band was playing "Sentimental Journey," we were on the boat pulling out of the harbor.

We were thirty days on the Pacific Ocean on a crowded ship. About half of us slept on the deck, and it rained nearly every night. The only good thing we had was hot bread and butter about 3 A.M. We would smell the bread baking and go to the galley, where we had some buddies. They would give us hot bread and butter, and it was really good.

We made an amphibious landing from about two miles off Batangas in the Philippines. We went over the side and crawled down the nets into landing craft.

And the damn war was over. It seems the Japs had quit about fifteen days after we left the States. I guess they heard old Hig had beat the Germans and was coming after them.

It was really storming when we made our landing. I lost my duffel bag and was lucky I didn't lose old Hig.

Batangas was the hell hole of the world. We went in looking for Japs that didn't know they had lost the war. I figured they would find out sooner or later by themselves, but I wasn't doing the thinking for the outfit, so we were the messengers to go tell them the good news, if they didn't kill us first.

We learned later how lucky we were. If the war hadn't ended, our division would have attacked the mainland of Japan from one side as a suicide diversionary force, while the main force was going in on the other side.

I heard that Freddie Fitzsimmons was coming to Manila with a USO show, and I managed to get a few days off to go see him. He asked me how I would like to come to Manila and manage the all-star baseball team from the other islands. He swung things to get me the job.

The first day more than two hundred players came to the workout, including Early Wynn, Max Macon, Jim Hearn, Joe Garagiola, Joe Ginsberg, and other major-leaguers. It took me a week to pick a team, and we began playing. In Leyte I picked up Vern Bickford and Roy Partee and a good little spider monkey for a mascot. We won everything in sight. We played a doubleheader on Christmas Day, 1945, in a series with a major-league all-star team, which we beat four out of seven.

I also picked up a Great Dane, and I used to put the monkey on the other end of the leash. The dog would take off across the infield, pulling the monkey. The monkey's fanny would get so hot he would jump on the dog's back and they would go through the center-field gate like Eddie Arcaro on Citation.

I was in Manila until March before I was able to get on a boat going home. General Reynolds, who was on the same boat, wanted me to stay in the Army and work in the training and athletic program, but I couldn't see anything but baseball.

I wouldn't take anything for my war experience. I met lots of really fine and brave boys. Some of them didn't come back. They gave it all they had.

9

Jackie Robinson

After the war, two things that hit baseball were education and breaking the color line. I think that opening up opportunities for education had more effect on baseball than opening the game up to Negroes.

During the war, millions of boys saw the value of education. They saw guys with good educations go to the top in the military. Most of them went through some kind of technical training themselves, and they saw what it could do to help you get ahead. When they got out, they could start or finish their educations on the GI bill.

While 1946 was the first year of good major-league baseball after the war, I think of 1947 as the end of what you might call the Babe Ruth era and the begin-

ning of modern professional baseball. That was also the
year we went back to Cuba for spring training and the
year that Branch Rickey broke the major-league color
line with Jackie Robinson.

A boy like me, who never made it through high
school, was the average ballplayer before the war. After
1947 very few came up were not high-school graduates,
and most had been to college and a good many had college degrees. The game is the same, but today's ballplayers are sure different from the rough-and-ready
guys whose only training was on the diamond and
whose only education was what they picked up traveling around.

I got out of the Army in March 1946 and was late
getting to spring training. It was sure good to be back in
baseball after nearly three years away. All the boys
were back that year, and we thought sure we would
win the pennant. In my opinion, the thing that beat us
that year was that Mr. Rickey sold Billy Herman to the
Boston Braves. At the tail end of the season we were
tied with the Cards and had three games with the
Braves. Billy beat us in two of them nearly single-
handed.

The last day of the regular season we were still tied
with the Cards. Most of our guys were hoping that the
Braves wouldn't pitch Johnny Sain against us, but I was
more afraid of Mort Cooper, who had come to them
from the Cards. Cooper pitched and shut us out, and
Billy Herman drove in the winning run.

The Cards also got beat that day, so we finished in
the first tie and went into the first playoff series in
major-league history.

Leo won the toss of a coin which gave him the choice

of deciding whether to open the series in Brooklyn or St. Louis. We went to St. Louis because he figured that if the series went three games we would play the last two in Brooklyn.

Whitlow Wyatt and I had been pitching quite a bit. I hadn't had but two days rest and he but three. I told Leo I was ready if he needed me. He decided to start Ralph Branca and told me to go to the bullpen and be ready. They got us out in the first inning and scored a run in their half. You could tell that Ralph was going to have a rough time of it, and in the bottom of the second they really got to him. With three runs in and runners on first and third with one out, I went in to relieve. I got them out without any more runs and went on to pitch four more scoreless innings. We scored two runs off Howie Pollet to make it 4–2.

In our seventh we had runners on first and third with nobody out, and Leo sent Dee Moore up to hit for me. He hit a line drive over the pitcher's head that was a sure hit until Marty Marion made the greatest leaping catch I ever saw and doubled the man off first. We didn't come close after that, and lost 4–2.

Our ball club wasn't down at all. Leo told us we were going back to Brooklyn and beat them two straight. When we got back to New York there were ten thousand fans to meet us at the station, and a big crowd spent the night in line outside the ball park. We all felt sure we would beat them.

Leo went with little Vic Lombardi, and Harry Brecheen pitched for the Cards. They jumped out in front right from the start and had us beat 10–2 going into the bottom of the ninth. But we came back with four runs and had the bases loaded with two outs. We felt sure that Howie Schultz, the next hitter, was going to tie it for us with a home run. He worked the count to 3 and 2 and then struck out.

Losing cost us at least $6000 a man, which would have made the winter more enjoyable.

I had a pretty good year, won 17 and lost 8 and pitched 211 innings in 42 games.

The next spring, in Cuba, the rumors started that Branch Rickey, now president of the Dodgers, was going to bring Jackie Robinson up to the Dodgers. He was a college boy that Rickey had hand-picked and brought into the minors and up to Montreal, the AAA International League, the top minor-league club in the Brooklyn organization.

We flew over to Panama to play minor-league local ball for ten days. We didn't have much competition, and all the talk was about whether Robinson was coming with the club. Some of the boys said it had to come, and why not, if he could make the grade as a big-league ballplayer. I was one of a good many who did not want to see it happen. We were in Panama when Mr. Rickey made the official announcement.

There were five of us that went straight to Mr. Rickey. All of us were Southerners—Pee Wee Reese, Dixie Walker, Bobby Bragan, and me—except Carl Furillo, who was from Pennsylvania. We told Mr. Rickey that we did not want to play ball with a Negro. He said, "Robinson is going to play for the Brooklyn Dodgers, and that is that." He said he had made up his mind. He said he would trade for those of us who did not want to play with Robinson as soon as he could make good deals. "But I am not going to make any foolish deals for you just because you don't want to play with a

Negro ballplayer." When we got back to Cuba, Jackie was with the ball club.

Pee Wee and I had an apartment together that spring, but Leo was staying at the Nacional Hotel and was married at that time to Laraine Day. He and Laraine invited Pee Wee and me to have dinner with them one night to talk to us about playing with Jackie. Leo said that he had heard that Mr. Rickey was going to trade us away as soon as he could make good deals, but that as long as he was manager of the club we would never be traded. He told us what a great player Jackie was and how he could help us win the pennant. Laraine told us what a great guy he was, a nice quiet fellow that we wouldn't have to associate with off the field. We talked for a couple of hours, but they didn't change our minds.

We didn't have anything personal against Jackie Robinson or any other Negro. As Southerners who had played ball up North for several years, we had heard a lot of talk about how we abused and mistreated Negroes down South, and we knew we never had. We had never had any race riots or trouble with Negroes in my neck of the woods down South, but I had seen and heard of plenty of trouble in Detroit, New York, and St. Louis.

We had several more talks with Leo and Laraine about it, but we were Southerners who had never lived or played with Negroes, and we didn't see any reason to start then.

During spring training Leo and Jackie became pretty good friends, and Leo was 100 per cent behind the management in keeping him on the club. We could see that he was a fine ballplayer and that he was Leo's type of ballplayer all the way—a real good batter and a fierce competitor. Before we left Havana, Furillo and Bragan changed their minds and decided they would play with Jackie. Just as we were leaving Havana, Pee Wee swung over to Jackie's side. That left me and Dixie.

We knew that Leo would fight to keep us on the club, so he was in quite a spot, and so were we. That was just at the time that Leo was suspended for a year. We didn't know who our manager was going to be, but Jackie Robinson was our first baseman.

Leo was not a Little Lord Fauntleroy by any means, but I do not know anything he ever did that was detrimental to baseball, which was the reason given for his suspension. There was talk that the real reason was that he was friendly with gamblers and was seen with too many gamblers. But wherever the team was, I knew if there was any gambling going on, and I never ran into the skipper at any of those places.

I have thought about Leo's suspension many times since 1947, trying to put the links in the chain, and I think the big link was Branch Rickey. He was an awful powerful man in baseball, and there wasn't much that he wanted to happen that didn't happen, even though he was looking the other way.

I have always thought that Leo got the rawest deal in baseball history. He was never anything but good for baseball.

Mr. Rickey was, in his way, good for baseball. He knew how to make money out of the game. He used to say, "I would rather trade a player when he has a good year or two left, so I can get something for him, than wait until he has started down the hill." Baseball is not a game of sympathy, and Rickey did as much as anybody to see that sympathy did not interfere with a successful operation.

He said he had promised his mother that he would never participate in the sport on Sunday, and he did not play on Sunday, nor did he appear at the field on Sunday when he was in the front office.

One of the Dodger pitchers felt the same way about Sunday ball as Rickey did and came to him and asked permission to stay home on Sundays. But Mr. Rickey said, "Son, you owe it to yourself and family to help the club in every way and every day you can. The only reason I don't come to the park on Sunday is because I promised my mother I wouldn't."

Mr. Rickey used to call the park on Sunday to see how many people had paid to get in, and he never refused his club's share of the gate receipts of a Sunday game. His strongest profane word was "Judas Priest."

We got back to Brooklyn and began the 1947 season under our new manager, Burt Shotton. When the season started, I knew I was not going to be with the Brooklyn Dodgers very long. I hadn't backed down on my stand.

I got more than a thousand letters from people down South calling me nigger-lover, wanting to know why I was blaying ball with a nigger, telling me I ought to quit playing baseball and come home rather than play with a nigger, etc. Those letters didn't have any effect on my decision. In fact, I wrote a few of the people back and told them I would be glad to quit and come back if they could get me a job where I could make as good a living as I was making playing ball on the same club with Jackie Robinson. I never got an offer.

If I could have looked ahead and seen all the change that was coming, I think I still would have done what I did. I was brought up a Southerner, and I was brought up to stand by what you said and believed in even if you were the last one standing there.

I loved Brooklyn and Brooklyn loved me. I knew what a great ball club we had and that it was going to cost me plenty to be traded away. Years later, when I was out of baseball, Dick Young, the sports writer, called me from New York and asked me if I thought I had a chance to ever be elected to the Hall of Fame. "Maybe you are just kidding me, Dick," I told him, "but I think I would have had a good chance if I had spent my first years with a better club than the Phillies and if I had stayed on with the Dodgers in my last good years."

I started one game for the Dodgers that year and re-lieved in another, and that was the end of my career with Brooklyn. I was traded to Pittsburgh on May 3—along with Gene Mauch, Cal McLish, and Dixie Howell—for Al Gionfriddo and $100,000.

Leo called me from California, where he had gone to wait out his suspension. "Hig," he said, "they sold you down the river like they did me. When I get back, you'll be with me."

Dixie Walker was "the People's Cherce," and Rickey kept him a year before trading him off. At least Dixie got another Series cut out of it.

The Pirates tied with the Phillies for last place that year, while the Dodgers went on to win the pennant without me. Jackie did a great job for them.

Jackie proved himself a big-league ballplayer, and there is no politics that can help a man on the field. One time Fritz Ostermueller was pitching for us against the

Dodgers in Brooklyn. Another Negro, Dan Bankhead, was pitching against us. Fritz had a real sweeping motion in his wind-up, but he swore that Robinson wouldn't steal home on him. He went into that motion with Jackie on third, and before he could look up Jackie was sliding across home plate. In the fourth, old Bankhead hit a home run off Fritz, and that really got him mad and taught him that Negroes were here to stay.

Sal Maglie and Robinson used to have some great battles. Sal had him hitting the dirt many times, and Jackie always found some way to return the displeasure.

Of all the Negro ballplayers I have seen, before or since I was in the major leagues, Jackie Robinson was the best competitor and hustler. There wasn't a base he didn't try to steal, including first. I saw all the Negro players in both leagues while I was a major-leaguer, and Jackie was head and shoulders above them all as a competitor. If it had been any other player than Jackie Robinson—say, one with less talent and hustle—the color line would not have been broken quite so cleanly and easily. His job was to be the first Negro ballplayer in the major leagues and to show the way for the others. He wanted that more than anything else, and he got the job done.

But I think there was one man who did more for the future Negro ballplayers than Jackie did, and that was Roy Campanella. He was next to Jackie as a competitor, but Roy showed baseball and all the Negroes that came after that you could be a competitor and a gentleman at the same time.

I was in New York a few years ago and went out to see Roy. It breaks your heart to see a big strong man like that sitting in a wheelchair, almost helpless. But he was in good spirits and didn't complain about the bad break that paralyzed him for life and cut his great career short. Baseball cannot possibly forget the big man.

10

The Traveling Casino

I wouldn't say the other players on the Pittsburgh Pirates led me astray, but I wouldn't call them a steadying influence either. The first year, in 1947, we weren't going any place in the National League race, but we sure had a lot of fun along the way. We loosened up pretty good most every night, and I am sure we did not lose any games that year because we were too tight. We won 154 and lost none in the night league.

The sports writers called us the "traveling casino" when we were on the road. We usually had a no-limit poker game going, and we played hearts, one of the sharpest card games there is, for a dollar a heart. Some of the players took their girl friends on the road with them.

There were no tears shed when I left Brooklyn. I was

told that Mr. Rickey wanted to see me in his office, but he wasn't there to see me. Burt Shotton told me I had been traded to Pittsburgh, and I never did see Mr. Rickey before I left. I was not surprised that he didn't have the heart to tell me himself, because I never thought he had a heart. I guess one of the things that made him great in baseball management was that he regarded players as property, not people. There was no room in any baseball operation he ran for sentiment. That's the way the game is played, on the field and behind the owner's door.

The Brooklyn ballplayers told me I was going to a club with power that would get me plenty of runs—Ralph Kiner, Hank Greenberg, Elbie Fletcher, Jim Russell, and Frankie Gustine. The first five games I started for the Pirates, they got me a grand total of three runs.

When Roger Wolff came to the Pirates from the Indians, he said the only difference between the two leagues was that there was more power in the American League. He started against the Cardinals next day, and they hit five homers off him in three innings. He said, "I must have been hearing about the wrong league. They didn't hit five home runs off me in two months in the American League."

"Don't mind that, Roger," Tiny Bonham told him. "You were just standing too far away from the ball after you threw it."

Speaking of the Cardinals and their hitting in those days, I once threw a change of pace to Stan Musial, who hit the hottest line drive I ever saw right between Hank Greenberg's legs at first. Hank came trotting up and said, "Hig, I should have caught that one." I said,

"Hank, if you had caught that one, it would have turned you inside out."

Tiny was our leader in the laugh department. I remember he was always talking about how live the ball was getting. "Hig," he said, "if you hold that ball close to your ear, you can hear that rabbit's heart beating in there." One off-night we were playing an exhibition game in Albany before a huge crowd that overflowed onto the field. One of the Albany players hit one into the crowd. So help me, as the ball went into the crowd, a rabbit ran out. "I told you," Tiny shouted. "That crowd scared that rabbit right out of the ball."

Billy Herman was managing the club. My only criticism of him as a manager is that I think we would have had a better season that year, 1947, if he had played himself at second. He was one of the finest ballplayers I ever saw.

The fans entered into the spirit of things at Pittsburgh. Every time one of our relief pitchers left the bullpen to head for the mound, the fans in the bleachers would offer him a dollar bill and ask him to go to a movie instead.

Often some of our players would continue their loosening-up right up until game time. Once when I started against Ewell "the Whip" Blackwell in Cincinnati, five of our regulars came to the ball park loaded. We went into the fifth inning 0–0. I had two out with the bases loaded on a walk and two errors. The batter hit an easy fly to center. Our fielder made a dash in, the ball dropped behind him, and all four runs scored. I gave the ball to Billy Herman: "Blackwell is hard enough to beat with nine sober ballplayers, but impossible with five drunks." He won that one 12–0.

Before a night game in St. Louis, four or five of us didn't get to the ball park until along about 7 o'clock, when we were supposed to be taking hitting practice. Dixie Howell, my roommate and the only catcher on the club that could handle the knuckleball I had started to throw, still wasn't there. When Billy asked me, I told him I hadn't seen him since noon. We were taking infield practice when Dixie showed up on the field, feeling fine. Preacher Roe was fielding throw-ins for the fungo hitter, and Dixie came charging on the field and threw as good a flying tackle on him as I ever saw in a football game. Just having fun. When the game started, Dixie retired to the back of the dugout and went sound asleep.

We went into the top of the seventh behind 5–4. Billy took our pitcher out for a pinch-hitter and told me to take Dixie to the bullpen and warm up. When he stepped out of the dugout, Dixie said, "Roomie, it is really dark out here." I told him to open his eyes.

In the bullpen I found out the only thing he could catch was a straight ball. We went in to work the bottom of the seventh.

I called to Frankie Gustine, playing third, and told him that if a pop fly went up either he or I, one, would have to catch it, not to count on Dixie.

As long as there was nobody on base, I could throw curves or knucklers until I got two strikes on a batter. Then I would have to come in with a fast ball so Dixie could hold it. Every time I threw a curve or a knuckler, I would see Dixie's fanny charging back to the backstop to retrieve the ball.

I got them out in the bottom of the seventh, and Ralph Kiner hit a home run in our eighth to tie it up. I got them out again in the eighth, and Hank Greenberg hit a home run in the ninth to put us ahead 6–5. The Cardinals had Enos Slaughter, Terry Moore, and Stan Musial coming up in the ninth. We got Slaughter and Moore, and I was two strikes on Stan and had to throw the fast ball. He hit a line shot to left field. Ralph Kiner made one of the greatest catches I ever saw in baseball, to hold the game for us, 6–5.

When I got to the hotel after the game, there was a message in our box for Dixie to see Roy Hamey in his room right away. I went up to Roy's room to see what I could do. Roy said, "Dixie was in bad shape out there tonight, and everybody in the stands knew it."

I said, "We won the game, Roy. Dixie will be all right."

When we got back to Pittsburgh, damn if he didn't go to Roy's office and ask for a raise. Roy told him he was going to send him so far from the big leagues next season that it would take a thirty-five-cent stamp to reach him.

When we were playing in Boston we often went to a Chinese restaurant where a good many show people came to eat. The manager was quite a ball fan, and I used to leave passes to the games for him. We would try to pay him, but he never did charge me and a few buddies for our meals there. We never did order any food. As soon as he saw us, he would come over and say, "Leave the ordering to me." They would start bringing the Chinese food out, and I am telling you that they would bring it out for about an hour. Damn if you couldn't have fed the whole Chinese army with the food brought out for us to eat.

One night after a ball game there were four or five good-looking chorus girls eating there between shows. I asked the manager if he would introduce me and one of my buddies on the club to a couple of them, and sure enough he brought two of them over to our table. They sat down and had a few drinks, and we asked them for dates. They said okay, but we would have to pick them up after their last show at 3 A.M. We met them, and let me say they were some dishes. We took them out and had a few more drinks and some sandwiches and a little romance.

We were leaving Boston after the game the next day, and we had not seen nearly enough of them. So this old buddy of mine and I decided we would invite them to New York, where we would be staying for a whole week while we played three games with the Giants and four with the Dodgers. So we called the two babes before we went to the park and asked them to be our guests in New York for a week. They said they sure would if they could arrange to get off from work. We said to call us as soon as they got to the hotel, if they could make it.

On the train going to New York, my buddy kept asking me, "Hig, you reckon they will come?" I said, "Hell, yes, they'll come."

After the first game against the Giants we went back to the hotel, and sure enough, the babes were there. It looked like we were really going to have some fun in New York that week, so I got another room. We made the rounds of all the night spots and good eating places that week.

I pitched against the Giants the second game, on Tuesday, and beat them 5–4 in thirteen innings. On Friday, Billy Herman sent me in to relieve in the sixth inning against the Dodgers to hold a 2–1 lead. I got them out in the sixth, and we scored in the eighth and beat them 3–1.

I didn't figure to pitch again that series, so I told my buddy to get dressed up, we would take the girls out for a real celebration. We started out about eight o'clock with a few drinks; then we went to a good steak house, then to a club for a little gambling and dancing. We got back to the hotel about 2:30 A.M. After my gal and I got to my room, I told her, "Honey, let's go have a nightcap with our buddies."

The door was unlocked, so we went in. Damn if my buddy wasn't sitting in a chair with this babe on his lap, crying like a baby, telling her how much he loved her and couldn't leave her and he was going to get a divorce and marry her and all that crap. I saw that he was serious. He had a fine wife and a little boy, and it made me mad as hell to see him acting like that. "I don't mind you having fun," I told him, "but when you start talking about leaving your family, you are trying me too far." I told him that if he didn't stop that foolish talk I was going to throw that damn chair out the window and he would be sitting in it. It made me mad as hell.

Instead of throwing him out the window, I started wrecking the hotel room. I pulled the shower out of the wall. I pulled the commode out of the floor. I pulled the sink out of the wall. I did a real good job of wrecking that bathroom.

Then I told both girls to go to the other room, and I gave him a little more hell and told him to go to bed and forget about this girl. I got in the other bed, and we both went to sleep.

About eight o'clock he woke me up and said, "Roomie, we better get up and get out of here. If you aren't a good swimmer, we are going to drown." Damn if the water in the whole room wasn't above your ankles and getting deeper. We went to the girls' room and stayed until time to go to the park.

After the game I went to the desk to get my key, and the lady said, "Mr. Higbe, you will have to see the manager to get your key." I went to his office, and he said, "Mr. Higbe, what did you do with the sledgehammer you used on your bathroom last night?" I told him I did it with my bare hands. He said I would have to pay the damages, and I told him to send me the bill.

My buddy and I took the girls out for a last fling on Saturday night, and we left Sunday after the game for a series in Philly on the way back to Pittsburgh. We never did see those babes again, but there was always more with the casino on wheels.

Word got around about my wrecking the hotel room, and Billy Herman called me up to his room when we got to Philly and said the sports writers wanted to have a conference about the incident. I told him I would meet with them. First thing the writers asked was if Billy was going to fine me for it. He asked them if they would put it in the paper if he fined me, and they said that would make it news. He said, "What if I don't fine Hig?" They said then it wouldn't be news. He said, "I am not going to fine Hig. The meeting is over."

After the writers left, I said, "Billy, why in the hell didn't you fine me?"

He said, "If I had fined you, it would have been in the papers and your wife would have found out about it. Anyway," he said, "when you get that bill from the hotel, it will be fine enough."

It was $765.

When we went to Chicago some of us would often go to a club called the Chez Paree to see the floor show after the game. One night a few of us went with one of our pitchers who was going with a girl in the chorus line. He said he was going to stick around and wait for her to get off at 4 A.M. When we reminded him he was going to pitch the next day, he said, "Who knows? It might rain tomorrow. If it does, I won't have to pitch. If it don't rain, I might win. So it looks like the percentages are all working for me."

Next morning about eleven o'clock I asked him how he felt. He said, "A little rough. I haven't slept any." He struck out fourteen hitters, drove in two runs, and beat the Cubs 3–0.

I went back with him to the Chez Paree that night. Some gamblers gave him hell for winning. They said, "After we saw you here all night and then go out with that beautiful girl, we didn't think you had a chance to beat the Cubs today."

He said, "Boys, don't ever bet against me when you see me out all night with a beautiful girl. I am just getting loose for the game."

In New York two of our players who were roommates went on a double date with two dolls, night-club dancing and having a few nips. One player liked the other fellow's date better than his, so he danced with her and asked her for a date for the next night. She said she was supposed to have a date with his roomie, but she would ditch him. They arranged to meet at the Diamond Horseshoe.

Next day his buddy asked him what he was going to do that night, and he said, "Roomie, I'm going to spend the night with a friend." He went off to meet the gal, who was wearing the same big black hat she was wearing the night before.

The other fellow dropped in at the Diamond Horseshoe about 10 P.M., and the bartender mentioned that his buddy had just left with a beautiful girl with a big black hat.

"He said he was spending the night with a friend," the roomie said, "but he didn't tell me it was a friend of mine."

In 1948 we started right where we left off in 1947. When I walked into the station in Pittsburgh to get on the train for California, three of the boys were sitting at the bar. We got on the train and went right to the club car to begin spring training.

We were staying at the Miramar Hotel in Hollywood in cabanas around the swimming pool. One of our players would come back to his cabana about two every morning and call for the rest of us to join him in a good-night swim. We would hear a big splash, and he would swim around the pool for about five minutes with his clothes on. He must have had some cleaning and pressing bill that spring.

In the morning, getting into the bus to go to the ball park, he would walk right past Billy Meyer, who was our manager that year, and say, "Billy, you've got to have that juice if you want to stay loose." He must have been the most loose ballplayer in the world.

Bing Crosby owned a good part of the Pirates, and he and all of his sons used to work out with us every day. We had many, many movie stars that came to work out with us. Some were pretty good ballplayers, but most of them couldn't hem a hog up in a ditch. They were swell people, and we had a lot of fun.

We went north and played the Giants in Oakland

and the San Francisco club in their park. We stayed at the Mark Hopkins and got in shape at the bar at the Top of the Mark. We didn't win too many ball games, but we were batting 1.000 in the night clubs.

When we went back down to Los Angeles for three days, another player and I rented the bridal suite at the Biltmore. Some of those Hollywood parties you hear about looked like Sunday-school picnics compared to the party we had. Just the suite cost $300, not counting what we ordered up, but it was well worth it. We really enjoyed our spring training that year.

We had a pretty good team that year, and I will say that every man on it put out 100 per cent on the field. We were right up in the pennant race all the way until the last three weeks of the season.

I relieved most of that year and set a club record by appearing in 56 games, with an 8–7 record.

Howell had been sent down, but we got another catcher that could handle my knuckle ball. He was another two-fisted double-shot-drinker. When I went in to relieve, the regular catcher would take off his gear and leave it at the plate for my catcher.

Bill Meyer called on me to start a game against Brooklyn. My catcher said, "Hig, I need a double shot and I'll be okay." So I took him to a bar across the street. His hand was shaking so bad that he couldn't hold the glass. He had to put his mouth down to the glass to drink the first shot. But after the first he got steady enough to raise the glass for the next shot. He got steadier after every double shot. It was quite a game, but he went all the way with me, and we beat them 3–1.

We went from Ebbets Field to the Polo Grounds and were called in to relieve in the sixth inning with the score tied. My catcher came out to the mound and said, "Hig, if you keep throwing that knuckleball, I will either become the best boxer or the biggest nut in the world." It was a real hard ball to catch. I threw it real hard, and I never knew which way it was going to break. That day I threw one against Johnny Mize that looked like it was going into the dirt, but damn if it didn't come up and sail right across the plate. Babe Pinelli called it a ball, and I went in to say something to him. But he put his hand up and said, "Hig, I missed it. I have never seen a ball do that before. Why do you want to throw a ball that the hitter can't hit, the catcher can't catch, and the umpire can't call?" We went fourteen innings that day before we beat them 6–5.

We went back to California for spring training in 1949, this time to San Bernardino, out in the desert a ways from Hollywood. One of the players and I began to go to Hollywood, about sixty miles away, every night after practice. He was one of the roughest, toughest men that ever played in the major leagues. We would get in about 5 A.M. and this fellow would be in my room at 6:30, looking like he had slept twenty hours instead of two, hollering like a bull moose to wake me up. My eyes were so red I think I would have bled to death if I hadn't kept them closed.

One night we stopped at a night club on the way to Hollywood and had a few drinks. Three big guys were picking on a little guy, so my friend said, "Hig, I think I will go straighten those guys out." I told him, "They're pretty big, so I'll go with you." He said, "Sit still. I can handle this."

He went over and said something, and one of them obliged by taking a swing at him. In a minute or two all three of them were on the floor, and he was walking back to our table with the little fellow, saying, "Son, you better stay with me so you won't get hurt." We didn't stay long, because we were asked to leave. If I hadn't been with him, I think he would have cleaned the whole joint out.

After ten nights of that, I couldn't hold out any longer and had to start getting some sleep. He kept on going to Hollywood during all of spring training, but he played every day and did a good job of it.

After working out, some of us would take the hot baths at the Arrow Springs Motel. You would take the elevator straight down to the hot-bath room. One time, while sitting in the hot room, Tiny Bonham was kidding Danny Murtaugh about how ugly he was. Tiny said, "Danny, you sit here long enough and your face will get as soft as putty, then we'll remold it." Danny said, "I'll try it. Anything would be an improvement."

That was the spring I took up handicapping in a serious way. I passed quite a bit of time reading the racing forms and then doing my handicapping. I placed my bets with a nearby bookie. I lost a thousand or more dollars before I bet $100 on a 12 to 1 horse which won. Since I was about even, I decided to quit. When I went to collect, the place was closed, and the people next door told me the law had beat me there and raided the place. I quit handicapping while I was still behind.

Charlie Grimm, managing for the Cubs, did a great relief job that spring. Five players from each of the four major-league clubs training in the Los Angeles area were invited to a big shindig at the Biltmore Hotel. Groucho Marx got each of us players up and gave us a going over with questions about how we met our wives.

He was really funny, and it was going his way until he came to old Charlie. They put on the funniest show I ever saw. Charlie stole it from Groucho, and we all felt pretty good that one of our people could stand up against just about the best professional comedian in the business.

We had just got back to open the season in Pittsburgh when I got a phone call at two in the morning from the wife of one of our players. She thought maybe I would know where her husband was. I didn't know, but I told her old Hig would get up and go looking. I knew most of the hangouts, and I hadn't been to about three of them before I found him sitting at the bar like he owned the world. I said, "Boy, you know what time it is?"

He said, "I am trying to drink enough to get the guts to go home and face my wife."

I said, "Wait until Billy Meyer gets through with you tomorrow."

"All Billy can do is fine me," he said. "I would rather face ten Billy Meyers than one wife. Someday I'll leave this club, but I've got to live with her forever."

Except for the war years, my wife and I had a pretty good time of it during my years in the majors. We didn't have any children, so we made arrangements in 1949 to adopt one. We didn't know whether it would be a boy or a girl, just like it was our own. I was glad when it was a son. We went to the hospital and got him when he was five days old and named him William Roy, after Billy Meyer and Roy Hamey. But when he got older, he wanted to be named after me. My brother had already named a boy after me, so we changed our son's name to

William Walter Kirby Higbe. Walter Kirby Higbe is my full name, although I have always gone by Kirby. I was proud that he wanted to be named after me.

On June 6, 1949, I was traded to the New York Giants for Ray Poat, a pitcher, and Bobby Rhawn, an infielder. Leo was manager of the Giants. He sent for me, as he said he would.

11

The Mighty 400

I am afraid I didn't help Leo much. I had a real good knuckleball, but he didn't have a catcher that could handle it. I wish he had, because I think I could have stayed with him for several years and been a big help to him. I would rather have pitched for Leo than any manager I know of.

I began to feel in my bones that old Hig was about through in the majors.

I went to spring training with the Giants in 1950 and worked harder than any spring I had ever been in baseball. No drinking, no smoking, in bed every night at eleven or earlier. I made talks at youth rallies and really lived a clean, wonderful life.

In July that year I was sent down to the Minneapolis Millers in the AAA American Association. Leo didn't tell me I was leaving. He had another man tell me. It was a sad day for me. When you are at your best, you think you can play the game until you are eighty. I wish I could have. I truly love the game.

I didn't have to go to Minneapolis, but the Giants asked me to go help the Millers win the pennant, and they would give me my release when the season was over.

There are major-leaguers, and there are bushers. Age has crept up on many a busher who would have made it, only there wasn't a vacant place for him among the Mighty 400. In my day that was all the places there were. The Mighty 400 have kept many a fine ballplayer from making it to the big leagues. Lady Luck plays a part but does not put you in the Mighty 400. Many a player with youth, ability, courage, and hard work was kept in the bushes until it all wore out. How many good shortstops passed their time away in the minors while Marty Marion and Phil Rizzuto, to mention only two, played 154 games a year, season after season? The same with every other position. In those days there were thousands and thousands of ballplayers in sandlot and semi-pro ball and in all the leagues from D to AAA putting the pressure on to get the job above and the one above that and to be a major-leaguer, and very few of them ever had a cup of coffee.

I have seen a great many good ballplayers in my time, and in my years in the majors. I saw some really great ones.

Starting with outfielders, there was Dixie Walker, my roommate while I was with the Pirates. Pitchers in the league used to call him the Magician. He studied pitchers the way a student does his lesson, and he hit the ball where it was pitched.

One year he had trouble with Claude Passeau. The next spring he said, "Hig, I have figured old Claude out. He has been breaking the slider in on my hands. I am going to stand a little further from the plate, and I will be ready for his slider." Sure enough, the first time we played the Cubs, Dixie got three hits off Passeau. I said, "Dixie, he will probably catch on to your standing away from the plate." He said, "No, I am only back two inches, and it will be hard for him to notice." Claude never did, and Dixie never had much trouble with him after that.

Dixie could really play the screen at Ebbets Field. I have seen many a batter hit a line drive off that screen and get thrown out at second by Dixie. The hitters got so they wouldn't take chances on his arm. He was a real smart player with a lifetime average over .300, and he could hit the home run off you when it meant a ball game.

And then there is the legend named Pete Reiser, the only rookie to lead his league in hitting until Tony Oliva did it in the American League a couple of years ago. Pete could really run. He once hit a hopper back to Carl Hubbell on the mound, and old Hub turned to toss him out as Pete was crossing the bag. Hub said it looked like he had been shot to first base. He could really go in the outfield. Nothing fell anywhere around center field, and he played fences like they weren't there. He hit many outfield walls going full speed, and he would hold on to the ball if he got it in his glove before he hit the wall. I will always say it cost us the pennant in 1942 when Pete hit the wall in St. Louis and got a brain concussion. What a great ballplayer he would have been if he hadn't run into so many walls! He is the reason they built the warning tracks around the walls in the major-league parks.

Paul Waner was supposed to be through when I came up to the big leagues. Lloyd was still with the Pirates too. Lloyd would get on some way, and the second batter would hit and run or bunt him over, and Paul would drive him in. Two great ballplayers near the end of their great careers.

Enos Slaughter, a fine hitter and outfielder, was the greatest hustler and competitor there ever was the whole time I was in the big leagues. He didn't know no other way to play than to play to win.

Another that played just about as hard as Enos was Phil Cavaretta, with the Cubs when I came up. Among the other great outfielders of my time were Joe Medwick, Jo Jo Moore, Bill Nicholson, Carl Furillo, Ival Goodman, Tommy Holmes, Hank Sauer, Johnny Cooney, Hank Leiber, and Ralph Kiner.

But the all-star outfield of my thirteen years would begin, of course, with Stan Musial. He hit over .400 when he came up toward the end of the 1941 season, and we knew then that he was going to be a great ballplayer. He could run and was a real good fielder with an arm that was plenty adequate. You could throw him one pitch and he would look bad on it, throw it again and he would lay the wood to it.

His only weakness was low behind. But he was one hitter we learned not to knock down, because it just made him mad and a better hitter, if that was possible. He must have hit .500 against us at Ebbets Field. He did a great job at first base too.

In center field, I have to take Terry Moore. He wasn't the best hitter I ever saw, but he did a good job with men on base. He might not drive in a hundred runs, but he would save you that many with his play in center field. He played right behind second base to haul down those line drives and went back up against the wall to get the long drives. He was the greatest defensive outfielder of my time. I never saw Tris Speaker, but he couldn't have been any better defensively than Terry.

None other than Mel Ott in right field. A good fielder, and what an arm! I never saw him make a mistake in playing the right-field wall at the Polo Grounds. A runner trying to go from first to third on a single to right was a dead duck.

As a hitter, Ott would drive in a hundred or more runs every year. When you started to pitch to him, he would raise his right leg. I thought he could be fooled with a change of pace. I threw him two, one a home run and the other a line shot off the wall in right that must have moved the stands back a few feet. He did everything well on a ball field.

I look around the infield and see many more great players. At third there was Stan Hack, who most of us thought had the best eye in baseball. The pitchers thought he was his own umpire. If he didn't swing, the umpire figured it must be a ball. And Cookie Lavagetto was a fine third baseman and quite a hitter.

At shortstop, who covered the ground better than Marty Marion, the Octopus? Billy Jurges was one-third of one of the best double-play combos of all time— Jurges to Herman to Grimm. And Eddie Miller could do everything well in the field.

At second base, Red Schoendienst was one of the finest ballplayers you would ever want to see, and a gentleman on and off the field. You can't say too many good things about Red. I roomed with Lonnie Frey while I was at spring training with the Cubs. That little guy put the fastest tag on a runner than anybody ever saw, was quick on the double play, and hard to strike out. For his hitting and base-running, Jackie Robinson ranked with the best.

At first base, Big Jawn Mize was not a great fielder, but what a hitter! Rip Collins was a fancy fielder and a good power hitter. I didn't see Charlie Grimm, but from what I heard he must have been one of the greatest.

My all-star infield has Whitey Kurowski at third base. His hands were fast, sure, and strong. In one of the key games the Cardinals beat us in 1942, Whitey caught and stopped everything that came his way and drove in two of their three runs. The next day we had a 1–0 lead in the eighth with Whitlow Wyatt pitching against Mort Cooper. Whitey hit a two-run homer that beat us 2–1. He was their big man that year and for a long time afterward, the best pressure ballplayer around.

Shortstop is the toughest to pick. I have to take Pee Wee Reese over Marion on his offensive value. He was much underrated as a hitter, by himself as well as others. He could cover the real estate on the left side of the infield and was a great double-play man.

One time, against Vern Olsen of the Cubs, Leo sent Pee Wee up to "look for the curve ball and spit at the fast ball." Pee Wee took three straight strikes and came back and said, "Well, Skipper, I spit on all them fast balls. He forgot to throw me a curve." But later in the game he hit a home run that won it for us.

Billy Herman stood out at second base over any other I ever saw. He played the hitters better than any second baseman—or infielder, for that matter—that I ever saw. He was the greatest hit-and-run man in baseball, then or now.

In one of those throwing contests that developed between us and the Cubs, Billy got knocked down on three pitches and got up to hit a home run and win the game. If Rickey hadn't traded Billy to the Braves that season, we would have beat the Cardinals by ten games in 1942.

There is nobody at first in my book but Dolph Camilli, even though I share with others great admiration for Mize. Though Dolph had plenty of power and drove in lots of runs, he was not the hitter Mize was, but Mize couldn't carry Dolph's glove. I have seen Dolph catch those short hops from right-armed infielders with his bare hands.

Once, in the twelfth inning against the Giants, they scored one off me and went ahead 2–1. Dolph, the fourth hitter coming up for us, said, "Hig, if somebody gets on, I'll hit one for you." We got a man on with two outs, and Dolph hit one into the upper-deck seats in center field.

The great catchers I saw were Gabby Hartnett, Harry Danning, Gus Mancuso, Mickey Owen, Roy Campanella, and Walker Cooper, all good country hitters with arms the runners respected. When you pitched to them, you never had to shake them off. They studied the hitters and were thinking with you all the time.

But my catcher is Ernie Lombardi. He was the best hitter I ever saw, including everybody. I could run faster with a mule on my back than Ernie could get down to first base. Even so, he had a lifetime batting average over .300. The infield would play him ten feet back on the grass, and the outfield would play him against the fences. You can imagine what he would have hit if he could have run a lick. He didn't get any cheap hits.

He could throw a runner out without leaving his haunches. He could rub up a baseball with one hand. He once offered to catch a cocky rookie pitcher bare-handed.

There were a great many pitchers in my time. For 1941, Whitlow Wyatt was the best pitcher I ever saw—and a good hitter too. King Carl Hubbell was supposed to be through when I came up, but he struck me out four times in a row on opening day in 1940, and I could have sworn I was going to hit every pitch. His screwball made a noise like a snake hissing when it went by you. I didn't see much of Dizzy Dean, my first roommate in the big leagues, and he had hurt his arm by then. I remember Big Bill Lee, Prince Hal Schumacher, Harry Brecheen, Howie Pollet, Max Lanier, Johnny Sain, Bucky Walters, Johnny Vandermeer, Paul Derringer, Claude Passeau, Jim Turner, Lou Fette, Lon Warneke, Freddie Fitzsimmons, Curt Davis, Preacher Roe, Sal Maglie, and Larry French—they were all outstanding in a great era of baseball.

My right-handed pitcher would have to be Mort Cooper, off his work over several seasons. He had a live fast ball, a fine curve, and a good change. He could put them where he wanted them and was a tough competitor.

Warren Spahn is my left-handed pitcher, great in every way. He was beating us in Pittsburgh 3–0 one afternoon, but we loaded the bases in the bottom of the eighth on a single and two errors. We had Elbie Fletcher, Ralph Kiner, and Hank Greenberg coming up. Spahn threw nine pitches and had three strikeouts.

You don't have to be a strategist to work with my all-star team, but here is the way I would line them up:

PEE WEE REESE, SS

BILLY HERMAN, 2B

STAN MUSIAL, LF

MEL OTT, RF

ERNIE LOMBARDI, C

DOLPH CAMILLI, 1B

WHITEY KUROWSKI, 3B

TERRY MOORE, CF

MORT COOPER, P

WARREN SPAHN, P

My manager would be Leo Durocher. He could handle players better than any other. He knew no two were alike; some needed a pat on the back, others a kick in the fanny. He knew what to do to make each player give his best.

It is hard to remember everybody you ever saw, and I may have left out some that were among the real great ones.

They were all different, but all alike in their love of the game.

When Spahn came through Columbia with the old Milwaukee Braves a few years ago, I said, "Spahnie, when are you going to quit and give the young boys a chance?" He said, "Hig, they will have to tear this uniform off my back."

I remember Paul Waner saying one time that he had been a holdout each of his twenty years in baseball. He said, "The truth of the matter is I would have played for nothing." That is the way all the great ballplayers were in those days.

12

Getting Them Out

When I was pitching for Brooklyn under Leo, we used to go over the opposing line-up before almost every game. The good reason for this was that no two pitchers who are any good will pitch a ball club the same way, and how a pitcher is going to pitch determines how the other players are going to field their positions. Once you told your players how you were going to pitch each batter, that is the way you had to pitch him. And that is why control is important. If you say you are going to pitch a batter inside, you had better be able to get the ball inside.

Suppose you were playing the Cardinals of the early 1940s, one of the best ball clubs ever assembled. Leo would give me a card with their line-up on it, and he would keep one.

Red Schoendienst, their lead-off man, was a good

hitter and a great base-runner. He was what we called a slap hitter, not very much power but a good eye, wouldn't go after many bad balls, would just try to lay the bat on the ball. I would try to overpower Red, get him out with a fast ball. You had to play him straight away, every fielder in his natural position.

Terry Moore, the next batter, wasn't considered too good a hitter. If there were men on base, I would pitch him low curve balls, trying to get him to hit on the ground into a double play. If there were no men on base, I would pitch the ball in on his fist to the handle of the bat. I would always try to get that first pitch in the strike zone. I would try to get ahead of Moore, then pitch him outside. The fielders would play him about three steps toward third base.

Now we come to the power hitters, and you have to be more careful. We've got Musial up there, one of the best hitters the game has ever known. He can hurt you with a ground single or a long drive out of the park.

(Another pitcher once asked me who I would rather pitch to, Musial or Kiner. If a single would beat me, I would rather pitch to Kiner, but if it took a home run, I would rather pitch to Stan.)

Against Stan, I tried to move the ball around—outside, inside, low, high, a good fast ball, a good curve, maybe a change-up, but never the same pitch twice. The best way to pitch to Stan was to bear down on the weaker hitters that came up before him. The real good hitters are going to get their base hits anyway, but they can't hurt you too bad if there is nobody on base when they come up. Stan hit to all fields, but we played him to his power, around toward first base.

The next batter, John Mize, had great power and was

the best low-ball hitter in baseball. I tried to pitch him up and in. In 1941, in a game for the lead, I told Babe Pinelli, the home-plate umpire, that I was going to pitch John on the inside of the plate between his belt and his letters, so give me the corner. My control was exceptionally good that day, and I got him out three times. The one hit he got didn't hurt us. Another time, when John was with the Giants, I had two strikes on him in a game at the Polo Grounds. Leo got one of his hunches and had Charlie Dressen give me the curve-ball sign. I shook my head three times. Leo came stomping out to the mound and said, "Hig, I want you to throw him a good overhanded curve." I said, "Leo, if I get that curve down below his belt, it will be kitty bar the door." I threw a good curve. John hit it all the way over the stands in right field, clear out of the ball park.

Another time at the Polo Grounds, Leo told me to walk Mel Ott to get to Babe Young, with a man on second and two outs, bottom of the tenth, score tied 1–1. I told Leo I would rather pitch to Ott than to Young. Although Ott was a better hitter, I had had more success getting him out than Young, just one of those things. Leo agreed. He had hardly got back to the bench when Ott hit a line drive through my legs, and the game was lost. When we were walking back to the clubhouse Leo said, "Hig, I lost that one, and you lost this one. That makes us even." I told him, "I believe the record book will show that Higbe lost them both."

Mize was strictly a pull hitter, and the fielders played him toward first base.

Number 5 was Enos Slaughter, and he could really fly down those base paths. I would try to pitch him from the belt up with fast balls, the first just above the belt, and go up on him to try to get him to chase a bad high ball, and then break him a good overhand curve ball down below his knees. The pattern was to set him up for the low curve with high fast balls. We had to play him straightaway because he hit the ball where it was pitched, outside pitches to left field, inside to right.

The next man was another great power hitter, Walker Cooper. He liked the ball over the plate, where he could get the good part of the bat on the ball. He especially liked it belt-high to his letters. I would try to make him go for a bad high ball inside and then go away from him with a good curve ball. We had to play him to pull.

Whitey Kurowski was the best seventh-place hitter in baseball. You would really have to crowd him and jam a good fast ball on his fist, never letting the ball get away from him so he could get the wood on it. We would play him to pull, all fielders around to the left side, which meant I had to be sure to get the ball on the inside. Otherwise, he would have a base hit to the opposite field.

When you came to hitters like Marty Marion, one of the best shortstops there ever was, most managers would say, "Just don't walk him." You didn't want him on base to give the pitcher a chance to bunt him into scoring position. You couldn't just lob the ball over. I gave Marty good stuff, fast balls and curves. We played him about straightaway and not deep.

The Cardinals had three good hitting pitchers in Mort Cooper, Howie Pollet, and Harry Brecheen. You had to bear down against them. Most pitchers are high-ball hitters, so you would throw them either bad high balls or good low curves.

The general rule I followed with pinch-hitters was not to give them anything slow to hit, because they are getting off the bench cold and cannot get around so good on fast balls.

If you don't have good control, there is no use telling your club how you are going to pitch. Many base hits are balls that would have been caught if the fielders hadn't moved out of position to play a pitch that did not go where the pitcher wanted it.

13

The Good (Bad) Old Days

It was about sunset for Babe Ruth when he was on the road with the Boston Braves and went into the diner for breakfast. He called for a double order of ham and eggs and fried potatoes and toast. But first he wanted a pitcher of ice and a quart of ginger ale. He poured the ginger ale over the ice, and he poured a pint of bourbon over that and drank it down. That was his fruit juice. Mike Gazella was there and told me.

When I was playing, there were some rough-and-tumble guys. They would go into a barroom and just as soon wreck it as drink a beer. Quite a few did tear the barrooms up pretty good. We always paid the damage.

When I was in the major leagues, I believe players were personally tougher than they are now. There were three or four teams we played, when I was with the

Dodgers, that we would always have a free-for-all with, or come close to it, every time we played them. Now you hardly ever see any of the teams have much trouble. We were ready for trouble all the time. Those throwing contests we used to have, knock each other down, could have been the cause of some of the trouble. Now, if you come close to a hitter, you have to apologize.

I remember the first year the president of the league sent umpires around explaining the new rule that you couldn't brush anybody back from the plate or knock anybody down. Larry Goetz had a meeting with the Dodgers to explain the new rule to us. I remember Leo saying, "Larry, there isn't a way in the world you can prove a pitcher is throwing at a hitter. How in hell can you read a pitcher's mind?" Maybe it can't be proved, but everybody in baseball knows that the knockdown pitch is—or was, anyway—as important to a pitcher as a saw and hammer is to a carpenter.

I have known pitchers who would throw at a hitter if he hit a long foul. Many a manager has come out to me and said, "Hig, don't let them take the bread and butter out of your mouth." Or: "Let them know you are out here. Show them who's boss." Or: "Knock somebody down."

You have got to be able to push a hitter back from the plate. If you have got a pitch that will keep a hitter from getting a toehold on you and beating your brains out, it's your job to use it. Baseball is a business in which you take care of your job the best way you know how. When you are playing pro ball, your living is at stake all the time. Are you going to let another man come and take your living away from you? If the hitter can't take care of himself at the plate, let him get out of the game. When Enos Slaughter used to slide with spikes high and separate the shortstop from the ball and knock him halfway into left field, he would explain, "This is a rough, tough man's game, son. If you are not going to give it all you've got, get out."

When I used to throw at a hitter, I would expect his pitcher to throw at me, and most of the time he did. It is up to a pitcher to take care of his players. If he doesn't knock a man down out of fear somebody will throw at him, he isn't worth a damn.

I never did throw at a hitter to hit him, except to plunk a few in the ribs. When I did, I would expect the batter to come charging out at me with a bat. When they do that, the only thing you can do is flatten them again next time they come up to hit, so they know you are not afraid of them.

Most pitchers agree that it is almost impossible to throw at a hitter's head and hit him, and most hitters will tell you the same thing. Eddie Stanky used to invite the pitchers to throw at him: "You couldn't hit me with a handful of buckshot." The only times I ever saw Eddie get hit were when he was trying to get hit, and there were a good many others who would intentionally throw a hip in the way of a slow curve or change of pace. When you blew one in there close to them, they would most always get out of the way.

The rule against knockdowns causes more batters to get hit than used to, because nowadays a hitter goes up there never looking for the pitcher to come close to him. So he digs in and is surprised when he sees one coming at him. Without the rule, he would be more alert.

Another reason many get hit is that they are guess-hitters. When a hitter guesses a curve ball, and you throw him a high hard one, it can be pretty dangerous for him. The pitcher doesn't tell the hitter to guess. Then some hitters will go up to the plate believing they can tell that a pitcher is going to throw a curve because of the way he holds the ball. Suppose the pitcher finds out about this notion—and things like that travel fast in baseball—and holds the ball like he was going to throw a curve and cuts loose with a fast ball? Would you call it the pitcher's fault when the batter gets hit?

I was pitching against Frank McCormick of the Reds in Cincinnati at a time when he had set, or was about to, the National League record for consecutive games. His first time up he had hit a double off a sidearm curve. This time I threw him a sidearm fast ball, intending to get it inside so he would hit it on the handle of the bat. Off my motion, he was looking for the curve, and he stepped into the ball too much. It hit him a glancing blow behind the ear. They took him to the hospital. The fans were wild enough to come down on the field after me. But he was back on the field next day, and his streak was not broken. I was glad he was not hurt.

They talk about how dangerous throwing at hitters is. How many professional ballplayers in the thousands and thousands of games played since they've been keeping records have been killed or seriously hurt by pitched balls? I don't know the count, but it is very few.

I can think of more pitchers that have been seriously hurt by batted balls than I can of batters that have been hurt by pitched balls. The hitters don't try to hit the ball to left or to right to keep from hitting the pitcher. More often it's the opposite—up the middle. The pitcher is supposed to be able to take care of himself out there.

I saw Hank Greenberg flatten two pitchers in two days with line drives. The first day Hal Gregg was pitching for the Dodgers, and Hank hit a line drive right back at him. Hal just did get his glove up in front of his face, or the ball would have smashed it to pulp. It knocked him flat on his back, and he told me the next day he was sore all over.

The next day Hank hit the same kind of drive at Harry Taylor, with the same results. Nobody said, "Excuse me," or anything like that. In fact, everybody laughed about it, but those boys came closer to getting killed than any hitter I ever saw. When Herb Score got hit by the line drive off Gil McDougald's bat, it was just an accident, but Herb was never the same after that. After Jim Turner got hit in the jaw by a line drive in Boston, he had to eat through a straw for weeks because his jaw was broken in several places. I have been hit by batted balls on every part of my body but the bottoms of my feet, and so have most pitchers who have been around a while, but we are supposed to be able to take care of ourselves. Getting hit by drives up the middle is just an occupational hazard. Why isn't it the same way for the hitters? They are supposed to be able to get out of the way of a ball.

The trend in favor of the hitter began when they banned the spitball. There were just a few guys that threw it, most of the time an old-timer trying to get by the best way he could. Players used to tell me to throw the spitter. They would say, "Hig, with your knuckleball, they would never know you were throwing it."

I never did throw a spitter because I think the knuckler is a better pitch. Even the pitcher doesn't know which way a good knuckler is going to break, let alone the hitter. It's a wonder the hitters don't try to get the league to ban the knuckler and put in a rule permitting the hitter to tell the pitcher where to throw the ball.

Outlawing the knockdown pitch was just plain discrimination against the pitcher and baseball. It's the big reason it takes so long to play a game now. We often played games in an hour and a half to an hour and three-quarters. Two hours used to be a long game. Now it's news. But today most pitchers are afraid to get the ball over the plate, and they are 3 and 1, or 3 and 2, on almost every hitter. The batters wear helmets and take a toehold, and the pitchers are afraid to get the ball over the plate. When you could brush a hitter back or knock him down, and he knew it, you could also get in there with the quick strikes. The winning pitchers are the ones that get ahead of the batters.

When the manager would come out and tell me to walk a man, I often used to say, "Skip, how about knocking him down four times, so I don't have to waste any pitches?"

I think it is harder to pitch today than it ever was before in baseball. You can argue that there aren't any more .300 hitters than there used to be, but look at the home-run hitters there are today. Everybody digs in and goes for the long one. It's like Ralph Kiner told Danny Murtaugh, "Get down on the end of the bat where the Cadillacs are."

Today's players know where the money is, and they go after it. They are a lot smarter than we were in many ways. Most of them get started in some business while they are still in baseball, and they save and invest their money.

A major-league coach I used to know as a player told me, "Hig, these guys that play today are so tight that they will go into a bar looking for a good-looking girl and sip on one beer half the night." In our day, if a ballplayer stood at a bar for an hour, his bill would probably be $75 or $100.

I was making $2500 a year when I went into the majors. Before I was through, the minimum salary was $5000, and today it is $7000. Then there were very few players making $50,000. Now that is within the reach of a good many. Untried rookies get big money just to sign a contract.

I am all for the ballplayer. I like to see him get all he can, because he does not have much time to make it, and he pays heavy income taxes as his salary goes up. The average big-league ballplayer is in the majors four and a half years, but he pays taxes at the same rate as the man who can expect a lifetime career at that level. All professional athletes are through or going downhill fast after thirty-five and should be given a chance to keep more of their peak earnings.

When we started the pension plan for players in 1946, there were a good many players against it, and we had to talk them into coming along with it. Originally, a player who had been in the league five years would get $10 a month for each year he had been in the league—$50 for five years, up to $100 for ten years or more. As the fund accumulated, the players have voted to raise payments several times. Players of my time were included in the first two raises but not in the last few times. It wouldn't have cost them a dime to include us, but I guess they figured we didn't contribute to television so why should we share in it. They will all be retired before long and will lose their say in it, just as we did who started it.

Most of today's players have been to college, and many are college graduates. They can and should go to college and get their educations by playing either baseball or football before playing pro ball. We used to say that the minor leagues in baseball was a place to be rotten in. College is a better place for young players to be rotten in than we had in my time.

I have wished a thousand times I had not quit school without at least a high-school education. I have talked to a good many boys who are prospects for professional ball, and I tell them all to finish college before they sign for professional ball. Some say they will play ball and finish college at the same time, but I have not seen a one that did it, except a few that got degrees over and above their regular college degrees. Very few boys who sign contracts ever make it to the major leagues, and if you don't get there, you are wasting your time. I tell the boys to get their education and then give baseball four hard years and if they haven't made the big leagues by then, to go into some other business. If you have a college degree, you can always fall back on that. An education is something you don't have to carry on your back. They can't take it away from you. I am speaking from experience. I learned the hard way. Baseball was all I knew.

14

A Place to Be
Rotten–and Forgotten

I went to Minneapolis in July of 1950 and helped them win the pennant. Against Columbus I pitched the only no-hitter of my professional career, a 3–1 victory. Two knuckleballs got past my catcher for the run they got.

We got beat in the first round of the playoffs. Seattle in the Pacific Coast League still had about two weeks to go in their season. They offered me $1000 and my expenses out there to play the last two weeks and give them a look at me. I went. They offered me $5000 to sign and $8500 salary, which would have been $13,500 for the 1951 season. I told them I would let them know during the winter baseball meetings.

I went to St. Petersburg for the winter meetings and met my old friend Dixie Walker, who had signed to manage the Atlanta Crackers in the Southern League. Whitlow Wyatt was his pitching coach. We had been

together in the old glory days in Brooklyn. Dixie and
Earl Mann offered me $3000 to sign and $6000 for the
season. I had heard that Rogers Hornsby was going to
manage Seattle and that he was hard to play for. I did
want to be with my old buddies, so I went with them
for less money.

We had our spring training at St. Petersburg, and I
got in real good shape. When we weren't working out,
Dixie and Whitlow and I were on the golf course.

I pitched pretty good ball. Brooklyn came to Atlanta
that spring, and I beat my old buddies. My record that
year wasn't all that bad, but the management was more
interested in developing young pitchers than stringing
along with old-timers. About six weeks into the season,
before a game with Nashville, Dixie had to tell me that
if I didn't look real good they were going to have to
sell me down to Montgomery.

I felt pretty good warming up and thought I was
throwing pretty hard, but I guess it was like I heard
Gomez say when he was about through, "I am throwing
twice as hard as I used to, but the ball isn't going but
half as fast."

I could tell after the first three or four hitters that
I didn't have it. They were pulling the ball down the
lines and hitting bullets. When I had my stuff, they
didn't pull the ball at all. Both Dixie and Whitlow were
hoping like hell for me that night.

Here is the way Pierce Harris of the Atlanta *Journal*
said what happened:

> I recall the day Dixie Walker talked to me about
> Kirby Higbe's future in baseball. He said, "Higbe is
> worried. He hasn't got a dime. If he doesn't make it
> tonight, I am going to have to let him go."

He didn't make it. Along about the third inning, they batted him out.

I can still see Dixie making that slow walk out to the mound, his eyes on the ground, and I knew what was in his mind. Higbe stood there fingering the ball, then handed it to Dixie, tugged the bill of his cap down over his eyes and walked toward the bench—and into oblivion.

When old Dixie came to take me out, damn if he didn't have tears in his eyes. It was as sad a night for Whitlow as it was for Dixie and me. Two days later I left for Montgomery.

We had a good ball club and won the pennant and the playoffs.

I was getting a little too old for those all-night bus rides. Most of the time we would get into the next town around 5:30 A.M. and have to wait around the hotel lobby until 9 or 10 A.M. to get into our rooms. One of our outfielders figured out a cure for those all-night rides. He would mix tomato juice and beer, half and half, and drink about five of them. I stuck to the straight stuff.

I went back to Montgomery for the 1952 season. It was really rough getting into shape. After you get to be thirty-three or thirty-four, it gets rougher every year. I fought it all year on those all-night bus rides. You really have to love the game to hang with those bus rides every night. It is not easy to ride a bus ten hours and pitch a respectable game.

One night we were going from Montgomery to Columbia. I woke up about 3 A.M., and we were in Atlanta, 150 miles out of the way. I asked the driver if he was lost. He said, "This is the way I was told to go."

So I asked the manager. He said, "I came this way because it makes the players mad. They play better ball when they are mad." I thought I had heard everything. I told him, "Let's don't do this any more. I am getting too old to even ride the shortest way and pitch good ball."

The minors were different than when I went up the ladder so many years before, but as Doc Jorgenson, the trainer at Pittsburgh, used to say, "You better be good to people on the way up, because you will meet a lot of them on the way down." We had quite a few bonus players with us. When the manager got on them, some of them would laugh him off and tell him they got more for signing than he made in his whole career. In my day rookies were making $150 a month. These kids got from $25,000 to $100,000 just to sign. When we started out, nobody would help the rookies, but by the time I was going down, everybody helped them. Baseball and its players were changing.

I played with Montgomery through that season. We finished second and won the playoffs again, but we didn't draw well that year.

One thing I think would help minor-league attendance would be to have the ballplayers get out and meet the public more than they do. People will go to games when they feel they know the players or have met them. Each ballplayer ought to go out once a week while in his club's home town and talk to civic clubs and church groups. Most players don't like to do it, but it would be good for them, their club, and baseball if meeting the public were made a part of their jobs. Maybe some of the bonus-baby flops could be of some use after all.

I took another step down the next year, when Montgomery sold me to Rock Hill in the Carolina League. "Hig," I told myself, "give it one more year and call it quits." When I was a big-league player I thought I could play until I was fifty. Many ballplayers in my day didn't think too much about the future. The day of reckoning comes before you know it.

That was a poor excuse for a ball club at Rock Hill. They were buying players for as little as $100 when you couldn't get a good batboy for that. Rock Hill was a good baseball town and would support even a fair club. When we won two in a row, we would always have a good turnout for the third game. But our problem was winning one in a row.

We had a third baseman whose arm was so bad he would field a ground ball and toss it to the pitcher for a relay to first. He was hitting .250 and was, outside of me, our top hitter. Hitting .250 was hitting a ton on that club. I pitched and was the top pinch-hitter and did a little of everything.

We really had three clubs—one coming, one going, and one there. Many of the players were making $100 a month at a time when most minor leagues were paying that much in meal money. One player told me he couldn't afford to take a girl out more than once a week, and then he split a Coke and a sandwich with her. In Charlotte we used to sign checks for what we ate. Several of the boys would eat and then order two or three sandwiches to go. I said, "How in the world can you eat three sandwiches after a meal?" They explained that the sandwiches were for them and their wives to eat when they got back to Rock Hill. No wonder they weren't hitting much. It is hard as hell to play good ball on an empty stomach.

The only reason there wasn't much drinking on that

club was because they could hardly afford a beer. They weren't much as ballplayers, but they were a fine bunch of boys and real good guys. They would give you the shirts off their backs if they had any.

The bus trips were worse than ever. I have seen better buses in junkyards than we rode in. They were safe. They couldn't go fast enough to get in an accident. We used to put boards between the seats to make a poker table, but the bus shook so bad you would find that the ace you had in the hole had been jiggled into a deuce.

We did have one smart player on the club. One night in our room he said, "Hig, what do you think about me becoming an umpire?" I said, "Hell, that beats playing on this club." He quit and started umpiring and has been in the National League for several years, Ed Sudol.

About the time Ed quit, the club business manager called me in and said he had an offer of $1000 for me from Forest City in the Western Carolina League. I said, "You better sell me. You can buy ten players for what you get."

Forest City was a pleasant surprise, a good ball club and a brand-new bus. My first game was a disappointment because I got beat 1–0, and I really tried hard to hit a home run to tie it up or win it. I finished the 1953 season there and decided to call it quits. Baseball had been my life for twenty-five years. I hated to quit. God, I hated to quit. I loved the game so much, and there wasn't anything else I knew.

A friend of mine, Red Simpson, was managing a semi-pro team in Simpsonville, South Carolina, in the textile league. He came to see me in 1955 and wanted me to pitch once a week. I told him I hadn't thrown a ball for nearly two years. He said, "Work out a few days, you'll be okay. We'll get you lots of runs."

I needed the $25. I had three days to get ready. The third day I knew it was going to be hell to pitch again. I was like an old firehorse. The heart wants to go, but the old legs don't move.

It was a Saturday night. I had to struggle like hell. The ballplayers were pretty good semi-pro hitters; I had known the time when I could have struck out sixteen to eighteen of them with ease. I had to work just to get them out. We went into the eighth tied 1–1. I told Red, who was catching for us, "Just get a couple on, and I will hit one out of here." Sure enough, with two on and two out in the bottom of the eighth, old Hig hit a home run, and we won 4–1.

Driving home that night, I thought about my years in baseball, how I had given it everything I had for twenty-five years. When you love the game and the fans, you have to quit when you can't give what the game demands and the fans want. When I got home I told my wife, "That was it. It's over." I couldn't comb my hair for a week.

On the way up, the minor leagues is the place to be rotten. It's your chance to learn and experiment. Not many people see or remember what you do.

When you get to the big time, you know you are good or you wouldn't be there. You cannot afford to be rotten. Everybody sees you, knows you, and remembers.

When the old body won't do what its mind and heart call for, the minor leagues is the place where worn-out ballplayers go to fade away and be forgotten.

THE WIND-UP

1

A Man of Letters

After I wore out as a ballplayer, I came back to Columbia and started out on the life of an ordinary working man. I didn't have too much practice for it. For twenty-six years I had played ball and been in a war and traveled far and wide and had become used to having fun and giving 100 per cent in competition. Nothing I had done since I quit school figured to help me much now, except the friends I had made. I am proud that I have always had good friends, then and now, and they have stuck with me. They talk about friends that fade out when things get rough, but that is not my experience. My friends have been with me all the way. All a friend can do, or anybody can do, is give you a chance. The rest is up to you.

I got a job as a clerk in the United States Post Office

Department. Anne and I and Bill lived in a nice apartment and got along pretty good. Bill was a fine boy growing up and a joy to us. Nobody ever loved their own born son better than we love him. I have told how proud he made me by asking us to change his name so he would be named after me. Anne had been operated on and had recovered, so that worry was over. My problem was never quite making enough money.

My first job with the Post Office Department was at Fort Jackson, part-time during the Christmas rush. You never saw so many Christmas packages as come to those dogfaces. About half of them were broken open, and we had to rewrap them. Sometimes there would be things left over, like cigarettes, candy, fruit, and cigarette lighters. I once told Ike Harmon, another clerk, that he ought to take a cigarette lighter for himself. He said, "Hell no, Hig! If I was to take one of those things, the first person to ask me for a light would be a postal inspector, and he would say, 'Let's go, Ike.' And before it was over, I would get three years for a three-dollar lighter." We would keep all the stuff that had fallen out, and the dogfaces would come in and claim almost all of it by Christmas. Their people would tell them what they had sent.

Then I got on working regular at the post-office annex in Columbia. Parcel post would be real heavy on Mondays, and I would help out on the delivery trucks. One route had more damn dogs on it, mean as hell, that looked like they wanted to eat you up. Mac, the driver, and I would take turns delivering to houses where the mean dogs lived. Mac would grab a package and head for the house, kicking at the dog, until somebody came out and called the dog off. Then it would be my turn to be attacked by those big brutes.

One old lady on the route had a great big old bull-dog, one of the meanest-looking dogs I ever saw. It was Mac's turn with an insured package the lady had to sign for. This big old bulldog came flying at Mac, and Mac pulled back his foot, ready to fight him off. The lady ran to the door and hollered, "Don't kick my dog. I had him castrated last week, and he won't bother you." Mac said, "Lady, I am worried about him biting me, not screwing me." Fighting off those dogs was about as rough as pitching to Musial, Mize, and the other great hitters.

They put me on the night shift, from 9:30 P.M. to 6 A.M., and I was pretty reliable, but one night an old friend I had played ball with in the Army came to town and called me at home at 8:30 P.M., half an hour before I left for work. He said, "Come on down to the hotel, Hig, we'll have a few short ones for old times." I was lonesome for old times. I said, "Van, I've got to be at work in an hour." He said, "You've got time to stop for a few minutes."

So I did, but the few short ones became many long ones. I kept calling the Post Office and saying I would be there in another thirty minutes. About 3:30 A.M. I told old Van I had better get to work. When I got there, they had called another man in to do my work, and it was almost time to quit anyway so I headed back to the hotel to finish up the evening with Van. Damn if he wasn't sleeping like a baby.

After that I went to work at the main post office, sorting mail. That was some hard job to learn. We had to learn schemes for the four different areas in town.

The red was the Shandon and outlying sections of that area, yellow was Edgewood, green was Northern, and blue was Downtown. There were more than a thousand streets, and you had to know just what block one carrier left off and the next carrier picked up. It was one hell of a thing to remember, and we had to learn all the districts and take tests. I say it was quite an accomplishment.

There were all kinds of interesting people there, just like there were in baseball and in the Army. We had one old boy who used to take his whisky to work with him in a medicine bottle. He said it was cough medicine. About every half-hour he would cough and take some more medicine and keep right on working. He had been doing that long before I came, he was doing it when I left, and I guess he is still doing it.

There was another old fellow that could also do a pretty good job of working and drinking. Every day before noon he would want to borrow $2 to get him a pint, and he would promise to pay it back by 4 P.M., and sure enough he would. We didn't know where he got the money until one evening he was having a nip out in back in the dark when a stranger called his name. "I'm over here by the tree," he called back. The stranger was a postal inspector who went over to him and unbuttoned his jacket. Christmas Seal letters with money in them came falling out for about five minutes.

Some interesting things happened in the six years I was with the Post Office Department, but nothing as exciting as playing ball.

A year or so before I left the post office, I was asked by the late Rex Enright, a good friend of mine who was athletic director at the University of South Carolina, to help Joe Gougan, his baseball coach, with the team. Coach Enright told me they couldn't pay anything, but they would give me free tickets to all their football games. While I was in Rex's office, I met his new secretary, Betsy Ains, a nice-looking girl who was separated from her husband and had three young children. I was in and out a good deal and finally asked her to go to lunch with me, but she said I was married and she wouldn't go anywhere with me.

Spring training had already started, and I got busy helping with the team. We had good pitching but our hitting was lousy. We lost a good many 1–0 and 2–1 games, some in extra innings. My heart really bled for those pitchers. It reminded me a good bit of when I was pitching for the Phillies. It seemed to me we could have got more base hits accidentally than we got actually. We only won five games, and two of them were practice games. Don Barton, the university's publicity man, said, "Hig, this is the only team we have had that will be strengthened by graduation."

I kept going into Rex's office every day before practice, but I wasn't hitting any better in the secretary's league than our club was on the field. But old Hig kept trying.

That summer I also coached the American Legion Post No. 6 team. We had a fine club and won 19 and lost 1 in winning our district championship. We went on to play Greenwood for the state championship.

Foxy Boozer was the manager of the Greenwood team, and he wasn't called Foxy for nothing. When we were going over the ground rules for the first two games at Greenwood, he said, "Hig, it looks like you are going to breeze through us in four straight games."

I said, "Foxy, if we are going to beat you so easy, why don't you forfeit the series, and we'll get on with the regionals?"

There were about five thousand fans in the stands and around the field, most of them with cowbells, fog-horns, and all kinds of noisemakers. They had my players not knowing what they were doing. I told them to forget the fans and to concentrate on playing, but they beat us 17–5 the first game and won the next two before my players got over the noise.

Before the fourth game, with us down 3–0, I had a meeting with my boys. They were playing Foxy's game by being friendly with the opposing players. Foxy had his boys smiling and kidding with my players, making them think it was just one big happy family. I told my players about the time Shoeless Joe Jackson was leading Ty Cobb by five percentage points for the batting championship when Cleveland came to Detroit for the four games that would close out the season. Ty and Joe were good friends, but Ty had figured out a way to beat him out for the championship. When they went out on the field for the first game, Joe said, "Hiya, Ty, old buddy." But Ty just looked through him and brushed past him. Next day Joe said, "Ty, what have I done you won't even speak to me?" Ty just brushed him off. Joe worried about it and got only two hits in the whole series, while Ty hit the ball good and won the championship. After the last game, Ty ran across the field and grabbed Joe around the neck and gave him a hug and said, "How are you, old buddy?" Ty said he thought old Joe never did figure out what had happened to him.

Before the fourth game Foxy said, "Hig, I wish I

were in your shoes. Your boys are good and loose and will probably beat me four in a row."

We beat them that night and the next night and went back to Greenwood down 3 games to 2. Next day at the plate Foxy gave me the same old story, but he didn't seem to have his heart in it. We beat them to even the series. As we went up to the plate with our line-up cards for the last game, Foxy said just three words, "This is it." They beat us 5–1, and we were through for the year.

The next year, though, with pretty much the same team, we beat Greenwood for the state championship and went on into the regionals, where we lost out.

Meanwhile I had been stopping in to see Betsy once in a while. After about six months I told her my wife and I had separated and it would be okay for her to go to lunch with me. But it was another while before she agreed, and I said, "Maybe my hitting is picking up a little in the secretary league." We had lunch a few times.

At that time I wasn't quite separated from Anne on a formal basis. But I was working at the post office from 9:30 P.M. until 6 A.M., working out with the boys before I went to work, and sometimes not getting to work until after a night game. When we played out of town, I would have to use up eight hours of my leave. Anne didn't know where I was most of the time.

After Betsy and I had been dating a while, both our divorces came through, and we were married after the Legion season of 1960. We had our first boy on Thanksgiving Day in 1961 and named him David Parks Higbe.

I resigned from the Post Office Department and went to traveling for a chemical company for about nine months, then with another for about a year. We had another son, whom we named Hugh Whitlow Higbe after my best friends in baseball.

I would like for all the boys to be big-league ball-players, for it is the greatest game in the world with the finest people in the world. But first of all I want them to go to college.

2

The Richland County Jail

I was out of work for some time.

Once I thought I had a good job all lined up with a big company. They gave me tests that showed I was suited for the job and smart enough to handle it. When I filled out the formal application form to complete the file in their home office, I came to the blank called education. I asked my friend who was helping me get the job what I should put in there. He said, "Our company requries a high-school education as a minimum, so put that down. Chances are it will never be questioned."

But it was questioned. They checked up and found I didn't have a high-school diploma. My friend wanted to hire me and knew I could do the job, but he couldn't get over the no-diploma hurdle with the home office. So I was not given the chance. You can be the smartest man in the world, but without that sheepskin you don't have many chances at the good jobs these days. Pretty soon I was floundering in debt.

I wrote some checks that bounced. When I wrote them, I thought I would get a job and make them good. I considered them more of a loan than bad checks, but things didn't work out that way. It came to the point where I had to get the money up or get sixty days in the Richland County Jail. It could have been worse, but Judge Powell was lenient, and I only got sixty days.

I spent one night in a cell. The next morning Captain Rawlinson came to the cell block and said, "Higbe, what the hell are you doing here?"

I told him my story, and he said, "Come on out of there." He gave me a job as trusty and a room on the top story of the jail, where I stayed with five other trusties. I worked like hell cleaning up and scrubbing the cells and carrying the trays at mealtimes and everything else I was asked to do. At the end of forty days, with time off for good behavior, I was free to go. Captain Rawlinson and I had become good friends, and he said, "Hig, I'll keep in touch with you. Maybe I can work something out so you can get a permanent job here."

He called me in about three weeks and told me to come to work, at first on a temporary basis. I got along fine, and he talked to County Supervisor Laney Talbert about putting me on permanent. Mr. Talbert said, "Jim, that is up to you." So I got the job.

Mr. Talbert has been in politics for a number of years and naturally has suffered a good deal of slander and abuse. Those who know him appreciate his loyalty to them and return it. He understood my situation and gave me an opportunity to work when I was down and out. He put his trust in me on Captain Jim's say-so. Their decision to help me opened them to attack by their political enemies, who were trying to defeat Mr. Talbert and get Captain Jim out of the jail. Nobody could have made a greater sacrifice than they made for me. All they had to do was turn their backs. But Mr. Talbert won re-election, and all attempts to remove him from operating the Richland County Jail and prison camps have failed. The good Lord takes care of those who look out for their fellow men.

The job didn't pay much, but my baseball pension would be coming in pretty soon, and I would be able to get by.

Captain Rawlinson and his family—Miss Pink, he called his wife—lived in an apartment off from the jail. He was and is one of the finest gentlemen that ever lived. He treated the prisoners real fair and helped them in every way he could.

The jail was built in 1914 and was a bad place to keep human beings. When I went there Captain Rawlinson had been working for two years to get a new jail. He deserves most of the credit for the new jail that was opened in April 1966. It's as pretty a jail as I have ever seen.

The old jail, where I worked, looked like a dungeon. It was built to hold 60 prisoners, but I have seen the time we had 150, anywhere from 15 to 30 in each cell block. The only paid help we had was us guards. We would have a detail of prisoners to clean the cell blocks every morning, but the jail was so old you couldn't do much with it. The pest-control man would come around to spray every month, and we would sweep up the cockroaches by the bucketful, some of them so big I would hate to try to kill them without a shotgun with buckshot.

The captain just did not have the money to feed the prisoners right or enough. They got grits and gravy for breakfast, dried beans and cornbread for lunch, and molasses and bread for supper. He did all he could for them with what he had.

We had four or five trusties that could go to town twice a day. The prisoners that had money could put in their orders for what they wanted—steak, ham, pork chops—and the cooks would fix it for them. The cooks were all trusties.

We used to have a cell that we called the hole. It was made out of nothing but solid steel walls with just a slit that could be used by sliding a bolt on the outside. It was black as hell and just as hot in there. When drunks came in raising hell, it didn't take long to sober them up in the hole. When prisoners got out of line real bad, we would have to put them in the hole for a few days with nothing to eat but bread and water. I have often thought it would be a quick way for some overweight ballplayers to take off blubber, but I wouldn't recommend it for myself.

One night, just before I was supposed to get off at 10:45, the highway patrolman brought in a big old boy named Lee, really raising-hell drunk. He was not a bad fellow when he was sober, and he wasn't ever in any trouble but drunk. We finally got him locked up, but he kept on raising hell, and Captain Jim said, "Hig, go back and get him shut up or put him in the hole." I knew it was going to be trouble moving him out of his cell. One trusty said, "Give me a knife, and I'll put him in the hole by myself." I was afraid he meant box instead of hole, so I went back to see if I could talk Lee into simmering down. If anybody had heard me talking to big rough and tough Lee, they would have sworn I could have sold snowballs to Eskimos. The next morning he couldn't even remember coming into jail, but he could have killed somebody just as dead as if he knew what he was doing.

At the Saturday-morning shakedowns we would always get a lot of weapons, such as spoons which had been made into knives as sharp as razors, all kinds of clubs, and razor blades. We would take blades and razors around twice a week so the prisoners could shave, and we would count every blade, but damn if every Saturday morning we wouldn't find a lot of them with blades.

One time when we were shaking down the colored block, one of the inmates pulled a gun on one of the guards. Another inmate grabbed the gun and probably saved the guard's life. We never did find out how the man got the gun.

Every Sunday the visitors would start coming at 10 A.M., bringing all kinds of food, fruit, candy, cigars, and cigarettes. We would have to cut into the cakes to make sure there weren't weapons or hacksaw blades baked into them. There would have to be a guard at each cell-block door to see that nothing was passed to the prisoners.

There was one trusty, Carson Pate, who became a good friend of my boy Bill, then about fourteen years old. Old Carson would generally just get thirty days for drunk and disorderly, but he got quite a few thirty-day sentences. Every time he would come back, my boy would say, "Dad, let's go fishing and spend the night with Carson Pate." We would go fishing and stay overnight on the riverbank. The only things we would take with us were coffee and cornmeal. Carson made the best coffee and cornmeal bread you have ever eaten, and he was a fisherman that I believe could have caught fish in a bathtub.

First thing, he would set his trotlines. Then he would get his fishing pole—no rod or reel—and sit on the riverbank and pull 'em in. Along about ten at night he and Bill would get in the rowboat and work the trotlines and pull in plenty more. The mosquitoes would damn near eat me up, but I don't think they ever bit Bill or old Carson, who were so busy having fun fishing, they didn't know there were mosquitoes out there. I would wrap up in a blanket on the bank, full of fried fish and hot cornbread, and they would still be out on the river fishing in the dark when I went to sleep.

There was one old man we used to have that came to see us for thirty days quite a bit too. He had a government check that came in the first of every month. By the tenth he would be broke and drunk and disorderly, and he would get his thirty days. With his ten days off for good behavior, he would be out again in time to get his check on the first. He had the timing just right. He told Captain Jim he would move into the jail if he could get out on the first of the month to pick up his check and get his liquor. Captain couldn't do that, but that's the way it worked out anyway. This old man used to tell me, "Kirby, I am going to wake up dead one of these mornings." And that's what he did. One morning we found him dead in his bunk.

The thing that hurts worse than anything is to see

young boys in trouble and to see the look in their parents' eyes when they come to jail to visit them. They always ask where they failed their children.

We had one kid whose dad would get him out before the key had been turned in his cell real good. The third time, the boy said, "Mr. Higbe, Dad will be down here for me in a few minutes, so let me sit in the lobby until he gets here." I would have done it but I wanted to talk to his father a few minutes. I locked him up and no sooner had hit the outer door than there was his dad and mother standing there. I took them into the back room and told them that he would be a better boy if they let him take his punishment. His father said, "That's what I want to do." But his mother said, "I can't stand the thought of him being in this terrible jail." A mother's love is greater than a father's love, because she has a greater capacity for love. It is tough for a father to see his child in trouble, but it is worse for a mother. I told them the boy was getting worse all the time and finally talked them into letting the boy serve his thirty days. He cried like a baby, but he stayed his time. That was four years ago. Today he is going to the university, studying law. He told me he didn't know what would have happened to him if his parents had kept paying his fines and getting him out of jail.

You hear that the boys who go wrong are usually from poor families or from broken homes, but I have seen just about as many boys from prominent and middle-class families in trouble. Maybe the difference is the well-off kids are pulled out of trouble and the poor kids are left in it. You never see people with money in jail very long. Talking about this, Jimmy Herndon, one of the jailers at the city jail, said, "You can't lock up the dollar for very long." Money and education are as good as keys to the jail.

We got one fellow who had served his term in the state penitentiary. There was a charge against him in a county in the upper part of the state, and we were holding him until the sheriff came and got him. He kept asking me to call and find out how much his bond was. The sheriff up there wasn't too interested and said to set it at $500. The boy said, "Mr. Higbe, I have eighty-five billfolds I made while I was in the pen. If you will get me out on bond, you can hold the billfolds until I get the money and pay you back." It would cost $50 to make the bond, 10 per cent of the amount. After I made the arrangements, he asked me to take him to a hotel where he could call his wife for money. "She will wire it to me, and I'll be able to redeem my billfolds in three or four hours." I took him to the hotel and told the manager to give him a room for the day. I watched him get in the elevator with his suitcase.

When I called the hotel at 5 P.M., the manager said, "Hig, that boy left the hotel fifteen minutes after you did. He said he had changed his mind about staying." The next day the sheriff called me and said the charges up there against the boy had been dropped, turn him loose. A few days later his wife called me to ask if he was still in jail. She said he had called her for money to make bond and she had wired $100 to him. That's the last she had heard from him. "Sell the billfolds and get the lawyer's money for the bond and forget it," she told me. That's the last I know about him. I took the billfolds to a wholesaler and sold them for $150. I guess he thought he was putting something over on me and his wife, but he was just running away from people who were trying to help him.

One man we had for drunk and disorderly almost broke down when I told him his wife was coming to pay him out. He said, "I don't want to go. I would rather stay here than face that music. She's the reason I drink in the first place." She came down, and there wasn't anything I could do but go back and bring him on out. She started giving him hell as soon as he walked into the lobby. I never heard anybody get cussed like she cussed him. She did not stop. She was still giving it to him as they drove off. I wished there was some way I could have kept him in jail.

We had all kinds of prisoners in jail, serving their time or waiting for trial for every crime you can think of: murder, rape, grand larceny, forgery—we had them. Some would kill you as quick as look at you, and some would never hurt anybody except themselves. Very few were guilty, to hear them tell it, and some of them really were victims of circumstances. Most of them were just uneducated. They couldn't get a job, and they would steal, lie, cheat, or do anything to get by. You would really feel sorry for them. You don't know what's in their hearts and minds. You don't know the troubles they've got.

3

The Losers

I was at the Richland County Jail for two years. I left because I believed I was to get a much better-paying job with the South Carolina Tax Commission.

I had worked quite a bit for Governor Russell in both his campaigns. The first time he ran, I traveled with Dick Anderson, who was ticket manager for the University of South Carolina and Russel's campaign manager. We were defeated by Governor Hollins in that campaign. But four years later I helped again when Russell ran against Burnett Maybank, Jr., and won.

So I believed that I would get the job with the Tax Commission. I told Captain Jim I was quitting to take this better job. But it just didn't work out, and I was unemployed for six months. That is the hardest work there is.

The Governor's executive secretary, Tom Hutto,

called me early one morning and told me to go see Ellis
MacDougal at the Department of Corrections. The only
job they had for me was as a guard at the state penitentiary, where I had played ball as a boy against the
Caged Tigers. The job didn't pay much, but Mr. Mac-
Dougal told me that if I worked hard I could work into
the job as assistant to Ted Petoskey, the athletic director. I had played ball against Ted in the minor leagues
and had worked with him when he was an assistant
coach under Rex Enright at the University. Ted, twice
an All American football player at the University of
Michigan in the thirties, was also a good baseball player
and was doing a real fine job at the state pen. (I applied
for the job as athletic officer there twice, but was ruled
out because of no education.) I felt sure I could do a
good job as Ted's assistant and told Mr. MacDougal I
would be glad to take a job as guard. I needed a job,
and something is better than nothing. It would be a
good bit like my job at the Richland County Jail, and
I had liked working with people who really needed all
the help anybody could give them.

I worked from 7 A.M. until 4 P.M., or until we had all
the prisoners counted. If the count wasn't right, we had
to stay until we found the one or two that were missing.
Sometimes a prisoner would get mad at a guard and
hide just so the guards would have to stay late.

Sometimes it would be many hours before you got off
duty. One time two prisoners escaped from a work detail out at the women's prison. The penitentiary issued
shotguns to about twenty of us guards and placed us
out in the woods surrounding the women's prison. I
stood in my place in the woods for hours, hearing foot-
steps all over the place, but the only thing I saw was
one lone little squirrel. I came near shooting him to

keep from wasting the afternoon and night completely. I couldn't believe that escaped prisoners would hang around the neighborhood very long. If they had liked the environment, they wouldn't have left in the first place. These two were picked up about two weeks later, far away.

Another time the sergeant said, "Hig, the fog is rolling in off the river, and we're going to have to put a tight patrol on the fences." I took a shotgun and walked about two hundred yards back and forth along the outside fence in fog so thick I couldn't see the barrel of my gun, let alone a man to aim it at. I didn't get off until the sun came up and cleared the fog away. All the extra time we put in was on the house. My pay was $200 a month.

Building No. 1 was built with slave labor before the Civil War. I have never been able to figure out how they got the big blocks of stone up from the river and in place. It is a big, dingy, cold place with five tiers of cells in it. The stairs were almost straight up, and it was a hell of a haul up to the fifth tier to start the counting. The bottom floor looks just like a horse stable must have looked in those days. There were two men to a cell, with an upper and lower bunk, a commode, and a washbasin. The showers were out in the prison yard. When that damn old building was put up, they didn't have plumbing. In that building you get a feeling of all the terrible and weird things that have happened there in all those years of men locked up for punishment.

The first few weeks my duties were mostly patrolling the yard and places where the prisoners were working, on watch to make sure they didn't congregate. We made spot searches to make sure they didn't have weapons or cash on them.

The department issued money made out of plastic, good for the things they could buy. But I wish I had all the cash money that is behind those walls.

After the first few weeks I was given a detail on the athletic field to keep the grass out and the whole area in shape. It has a football field, baseball field, tennis and badminton courts, and horseshoe pits—a really fine athletic facility—surrounded by an inner fence and an outer fence. My ten men were all good workers and, I thought, good fellows. They had from six months to life to serve. If one of them stopped to smoke a cigarette or get a drink of water, the whole bunch wanted to do the same thing. It took me a while to get used to their ways, but I finally decided to give them a ten-minute break every hour, and after that things went smooth.

Athletics was the best break in their lives. Every Saturday and Sunday the whole institution would come out to watch the baseball or football games, depending on the season. Teams from outside would come in to play baseball, as I had as a boy, and we also had a league among the work camps and the laundry. But football was limited to the prisoners, with the big competition between the laundry and the pen.

They would really bet like hell on the games. The officials were prisoners, and those poor guys were under more pressure than any umpire or referee I ever saw. They couldn't leave town after the close calls they had to make.

The football players hit hard, and there were some heavyweights among them. They played good football, and there were no sissies on those teams. I believe I could have put a team together that would have given any of the professional football teams a real contest. There were a few boys on the baseball teams that could have made it all the way. They had three days a week to practice and get in shape, after their regular working hours, and they gave it all they had on the field.

I used to spend time talking with the prisoners. They had their problems, like everybody else. They had excuses for everything they had done, like everybody else. You can't read a man's mind or see inside his heart, so who am I to know the truth? If we had all been caught every time we broke the law, there wouldn't be anybody on the outside looking in.

One boy that worked for me on a detail was in for armed robbery. He said he had quit school and had been trying to get work for a good while, but couldn't get a job that paid enough to live on. He said he started writing checks and was doing pretty good, hanging around night spots and shacking up with those good-looking babes. He got to like the night life. But they were getting pretty hot behind him, so he decided to rob a place and get enough to clean things up. But before he did, he ran into a boy from New Orleans who had a jewelry store cased back home. He went to New Orleans with his new buddy, and they pulled the job at midnight. He said he had close to $70,000 worth of diamonds in his pocket as his share. He sold them to a fence for $11,000 and ran into a nice-looking babe and went through it in two months. He was fixing to leave town, but they caught his buddy, who squealed like a pig. They picked him up, and he got ten years. He served six and a half years in Louisiana, and he said, "Hig, I thought I was cured. I came back home to South Carolina and tried to get a job at the mill and everywhere else, but they wouldn't touch me with a pole. They picked me up on a bad-check charge seven years old, and I got a year for that and served it out in nine months. When I got out, I just gave up and said if they won't give me a chance, I will take a gun and get all I can."

He was a small fellow and would hide in stores and wait until everybody was gone and make a haul and walk out like he owned the place. He said his biggest mistake was joining up with two other fellows and getting caught holding up a filling station. He is serving twenty years and is thirty years old. He has spent most of his time since he was eighteen in prison. You judge him.

An old man there had life for killing his wife. When I took my working detail out, I also took the disabled prisoners out and let them loaf. This old man said, "Mr. Higbe, I had been married thirty-nine years when my wife was killed. Do you think I would kill a woman I had been married to and loved that long? I used to have me a shack down on the river, and I would go down there and fish and would sell the fish in town. One morning I was up as usual way before sun-up and went to town and sold my fish and come on back home with the money and found my wife laying in a pool of blood as dead as those fish I had taken to town. They locked me up and charged me with murder. None of my children will come to see me or even write to me."

He got some kind of a pension check every month. He would buy all the boys on the detail a Coke, and damn if he didn't send all the rest of his money to a bank in his home town for his children and his grandchildren.

One of the damndest cases I heard the whole time I was there I didn't get from the fellow himself. The story went that he had caught his wife cheating and had chased the fellow for three days before he caught him and killed him. He cut his head off and took it to his house and put it on the mantel and tied his wife to a chair and said, "Here is the son of a bitch you love so much." She was in that chair for two days before anybody found her. She was stark out of her mind. He got life and had been turned down for parole four times before I got there, but he still thought he was justified. To look at him, you would never think he could have done a thing like that.

A good many years before I went to work there, five prisoners got the warden in his office and were holding him and demanding a getaway car and guns for their escape. They were armed with two icepicks. The warden's office was just two doors from a cell block we called Old Cuba, where we kept prisoners that were waiting to be tried for breaking prison rules. These prisoners got out of there and held him in his office for six or seven hours and worked him over with those picks. The Governor and nearly every other big shot in the state talked to them on the phone, trying to get them to let the warden go. When guards finally broke in and got him, the warden had five hundred stab wounds in his body. The five prisoners got the electric chair, one just a young boy with six months to serve.

They have in prison what they call prison industries, where they make clothes, furniture, license plates for the state and a few foreign countries, and other things. The boys make anywhere from 50 cents to a maximum of $7.50 a week.

They use this money to buy cigarettes and other luxuries. They are allowed to set tables up in the yard and gamble Saturday and Sunday mornings from 9 A.M. until noon.

For extra work, they can buy leather goods from the

prison canteen and make men's billfolds and ladies' purses. They sell the billfolds for from $1 to $7.50 and the purses for from $7.50 to $25.00. Some of the prisoners go into business and hire other prisoners to cut the patterns and stamp designs on them and still others to sew and lace them up. The prisoners that are industrious can really save some money from the pocketbook business. It's mostly the short-termers, the ones that know they are getting out soon, that work at it.

I believe that most of the trouble inside the walls is caused by sex. Money doesn't seem to mean much to most of the prisoners while they are there. You could trace almost every cutting scrape to sex.

I was walking into Building No. 1 one day and found a young boy, about eighteen, bleeding like a stuck pig from a jagged cut behind his left ear. He said somebody had stuck him with a piece of broken glass. He said he didn't know who. I took him to the hospital, and they sewed him up, but he never would say who had stabbed him. Another prisoner told me I was wasting my time asking him. But he said, "Sergeant, I won't tell you either, but I will tell you that he is a girl friend who got caught talking to another prisoner, and his boy friend sliced him a little to let him know that he couldn't cheat on him."

When a young boy came into the pen, the old prisoners' mouths would start to water. They would buy the young boys Cokes, candy, cigarettes, and give them money, just like any man would buy his girl presents on the outside. Some would even wear sweet perfume like a girl. You would see some of the toughest guys in the world walking hand in hand like a boy and girl taking a Sunday walk in the park. They would be just as jealous as a man on the outside would be of his wife. They would cut hell out of anybody that messed around. They all knew who the girl friends were, and most of the time the other prisoners wouldn't fool around with another's girl friend. But if anybody did, there would be some cutting going on.

Knives weren't hard to come by. They would steal spoons from the mess hall and make knives as sharp as any razor. Whenever we had shakedowns, we would come up with all kinds of weapons made out of spoons, which were the only utensils they had to eat with.

I used to think that the prison might have cut down on the weapons if it issued every man a spoon when he came in and told him he would have to eat with his fingers if he lost it, but that would probably only result in lots of spoon-stealing. I used to think that the officials might have cut down on all the cuttings by separating the queens from the rest, but they said that was impossible too.

I used to try to think what I could do for those poor devils, but it was like my dad used to tell me, "Son, you can't change the world, so just do the best you can."

The way I got into trouble started by trying to help a prisoner. He had a long sentence and a young family outside. He said his wife was going to divorce him and go away for good. He felt like he couldn't stand it in there. He couldn't sleep nights. He felt like he was going to go crazy.

I happened to have two Carbital pills in my pocket. They are a mild sleeping pill that I had a prescription for. I said, "Maybe these will help you get a good night's sleep."

Next day he said, "Those things really did help me. I slept like a baby last night. How would you like to make some money?"

I said, "Who doesn't want to make some money?"

He said, "I'll give you a dollar apiece for those pills."

I needed the money. My pay just didn't cover it. I knew it was against the law, but I couldn't see what harm those sleeping pills could do. I got 100 of them at the drugstore next day for $3.09 and carried them in. He was short of what he said he would pay, but I got $75 for them.

Another prisoner came to me and said he knew where there were 1000 of those pills and would give me $250 to pick them up at a certain time and place and get them inside to him.

I found out how to get them inside with a baseball.

I met the fellow at the time and place and got the thousand pills and wrapped them in cotton and adhesive tape and put them inside a baseball cover. I drove a boy at night to about a block from the fence and told him to go to the fence and throw the ball over both fences onto the athletic field. The next morning, which was Saturday, the prisoner on my detail picked the ball up and carried it inside through the tunnel after the ball game. The prisoners are not searched going from the athletic field back into the main prison after the games.

About a week later the same prisoner came to me and said, "This party has another thousand pills. Can you get them in?"

I said, "I guess I can."

He said, "Same deal as before."

I don't know how the outside party let him know that he had the pills and his when and where, but he was Johnny on the spot. I made my baseball and got my friend to throw it over and waited in the car for him. He came back white and scared. "Just as I heaved it over the fence, a police car came cruising. I thought sure as hell they saw me." I decided I had gone far enough.

But I got another proposition. This fellow told me another inmate would pay $100 for 100 pills as soon as I put them in his hand. I told him I didn't like him telling other inmates where the pills were coming from. I would get in trouble sure. I said, "This is absolutely the last time, don't bother to ask me again."

That was one time too many. About three o'clock next morning Mr. MacDougal called me at home and said, "Higbe, I want to see you down here right away." I said, "Can't it wait until later?" He said, "No, this is very urgent." I knew then that it was about the pills. But I went right down, and Warden Goodman and Major Merritt were waiting with him for me in his office.

They told me that an inmate had reported that I was bringing pills into the penitentiary. I asked him to bring the inmate up and face me with the accusation, but he wouldn't do that. They questioned me about an hour and a half, and I did not admit anything. Mr. Mac told me to come back after lunch and we would talk further.

I figured I had better call a lawyer, and the ones I turned to were Robert E. Kneece and William Otis Kneece. They were only thirty-two and twenty-eight years old, but already they have built a fine reputation as lawyers and they come from one of the most respected and admired families in our part of the country. Their daddy, the late Otis Kneece, who was in the real-estate business for years, was best friend to my oldest brother. Their second cousin, old Country Kneece, was one of the boys I first started playing ball with back in the days when it all lay before me. I had known Bobby and Billy since they were born and had done a lot of fishing and shooting with them.

They told me to get to their office right away. I told them I was guilty. They told me I had a right to be represented by counsel in all stages of the proceedings from then on and that I did not have any responsibility to testify against myself.

When I went back to see Mr. Mac, he asked if I would mind taking a lie-detector test to clear this thing up. I should have consulted Bobby and Billy, but I said, "Hell, no, I don't mind."

I went with Mr. Mac and Warden Goodman to the office of the South Carolina Law Enforcement Division. The lieutenant with the lie detector gave me a real Sunday-school talk. He told me that they didn't want to hurt me in any way but that I should tell everything so that they could get to the bottom of this. I didn't know how the thing worked, and they found out I was involved, and I admitted my part in the whole thing.

Mr. Mac said, "Kirby, call Bobby and tell him to be at Judge Powell's at ten in the morning. You be with him, and you can make bond." Judge Powell set bond at $1500 for me to appear in court in April 1965. I was fifty years old.

I pleaded guilty at the hearing before Judge George T. Gregory, Jr. A good many of my friends and the press people were there. Dr. Wyatt, who was with the State Drug Administration, got up and described the kind of pills involved. Bobby asked him if they were considered pep pills.

"No, sir," he said, "just the opposite. They are sleeping pills."

That was the only time I heard any laughter in the

court room. I guess they thought that old Hig was trying to put the prisoners to sleep to make his work
lighter.

Bobby told Judge Gregory about the hard financial
time I had been having. In his plea for leniency, he
quoted the part of the Lord's Prayer about lead us not
into temptation. He asked the judge if he could find it
in his heart to put me on probation.

Judge Gregory said that he had followed my baseball
career and had always admired me, that I had been one
of his baseball heroes. He gave me a three-year suspended sentence and put me on probation for three
years. He said he hoped he was doing the right thing.

Of course the whole thing was reported all over the
country, and all the newspaper stories said that I was
guilty of passing dope to prisoners. I can't blame them,
but it wasn't dope in the way people think of dope. I
knew that it was against the law and was wrong, but I
also knew that the pills couldn't cause any trouble or
do anything but give some of those poor devils, whose
punishment is worse than almost anybody on the outside knows, a few hours of sleep and forgetfulness.

I wish I had the money to buy a big business so I
could give some of them a job when they get out. They
come out with two strikes against them—no job and no
education. I think most of them would make good if
somebody would show a little faith and trust in them.

4

Another Game Tomorrow

Under the pension plan I was credited with thirteen years in the major leagues—1937 to 1950. I pitched 1919 innings in 400 games and won 118 and lost 98. I got 954 strikeouts and gave up 949 walks. My earned-run average was 3.66. Considering that I spent some of my best years with the worst teams in the league, it is not too bad a record. Anyway, it is the only one I've got.

If I had my life to live over, I would still be a ball-player, but I would also go on and finish college.

A fellow was telling me the other day, "Hig, but look at all the memories you have."

"Yes, some bad and some good, but it is hard to eat memories."

It set me to thinking. Since my hearing and going on probation, I haven't been able to find anything to do. I have my baseball pension of $209.93 a month. My true friends, Bobby and Billy Kneece, who are now handling my affairs so I can get on my feet and stay on them, have me come down to their law office and help out on errands and things that will save their time. They've got a library where a man can be alone with a pen and those big yellow legal pads of paper they use to make notes on and write drafts of their legal work. So I picked up a pen one day and started to write out some of the things that I have done and that have happened since I was a little boy, going back to my home and early memories.

Now the story is finished. Thinking about what I have done and the wonderful opportunities I had to meet people and to learn from them has given me new hope and confidence. It has taught me that the story never ends until you die, and even then some part of you goes on in your children and the people who remember you.

The way I feel now, tomorrow is another game. I am going to give it everything I've got.